P9-EAO-101

Ian Frazier

Author of the National Bestseller *Great Plains*

Dating Your

PICADOR

Acclaim for *Dating Your Mom*

"Bold, challenging humor that works as the inspiration for both laughs and thoughts."

—*The Philadelphia Inquirer*

"Intellectual knee-slapping . . . some of the titles alone are good for a hearty chuckle."

—*The Boston Globe*

"A satisfying and refreshing humorous voice . . . reminding us that there is nothing so sacred it cannot or should not be laughed at."

—*Los Angeles Times*

"Shows that he is one of our best contemporary humorists."

—*Kirkus Reviews*

"It's a treat to have this first collection of Frazier's as a mirthful refuge to turn to when a grim era's inane clichés start flying."

—*Newsday*

"Very, very funny . . . simple, graceful, funny pieces with no obvious targets. . . . Frazier's writing is so graceful and controlled that all these pieces have the feel of an effortless romp."

—*The Voice Literary Supplement*

"One of America's funniest writers."

—*Vogue*

Dating Your Mom

Also by Ian Frazier

Nobody Better, Better Than Nobody

Great Plains

Family

Coyote v. Acme

On the Rez

It Happened Like This (translator)

The Fish's Eye

DATING YOUR MOM

IAN FRAZIER

Picador
Farrar, Straus and Giroux
New York

To my brother Fritz

www.picadorusa.com

Picador® is a U.S. registered trademark and is used by Farrar, Straus and Giroux under license from Pan Books Limited.

For information on Picador Reading Group Guides, as well as ordering, please contact the Trade Marketing department at St. Martin's Press.
Phone: 1-800-221-7945 extension 763
Fax: 212-677-7456
E-mail: trademarketing@stmartins.com

Grateful acknowledgement is made to *The New Yorker*, where all of these pieces, except the following, first appeared: "The Museum," "List of Funny Names Released," and "A Note from the Playwright" were originally published by *The Atlantic*; "Your Nutrition & You" first ran in *The New Republic*.

Library of Congress Cataloging-in-Publication Data

Frazier, Ian.
    Dating your mom.
    ISBN 0-312-42152-4
    I. Title.
PS3556.R363D3   1986   813'.54   85-20646

First published in the United States by Farrar, Straus and Giroux

First Picador Edition: March 2003

10 9 8 7 6 5 4 3 2 1

Contents

Dating Your Mom

THE BLOOMSBURY GROUP
LIVE AT THE APOLLO
(Liner Notes from the New Best-Selling Album)

Live albums aren't supposed to be as exciting, as *immediate* as the actual stage performances they record, but (saints be praised!) the Bloomsbury Group's newest, *Live at the Apollo,* is a shouting, foot-stomping, rafter-shaking exception to this rule. Anyone who has not seen John Maynard Keynes doing his famous strut, or Duncan Grant playing his bass while flat on his back, can now get an idea of what he's been missing! The Bloomsbury Group has always stood for seriousness about art and skepticism about the affectations of the self-important, and it has been opposed to the avowed philistinism of the English upper classes. *Live at the Apollo* is so brilliantly engineered that this daring Neo-Platonism comes through as unmistakably as the super-bad Bloomsbury beat. A few critics have com-

3

plained that the Bloomsbury Group relies too heavily on studio effects; this album will instantly put such objections to rest. The lead vocals (some by "Mister White Satin" Lytton Strachey, the others by Clive Bell) are solid and pure, even over the enthusiastic shouts of the notoriously tough-to-please Apollo crowd, and the Stephen Sisters' chorus is reminiscent of the Three Brontës at their best. There is very little "dead air" on this album, even between cuts. On Band 3 on the flip side, there is a pause while the sidemen are setting up, and if you listen carefully you can hear Leonard Woolf and Virginia Stephen coining withering epigrams and exchanging banter with the audience about Macaulay's essay on Warren Hastings. Very mellow, very close textual criticism.

Lytton Strachey, who has been more or less out of the funk-literary picture since his girlfriend threw boiling grits on him in his Memphis hotel room in March of 1924, proves here that his voice is still as sugar-cured as ever. In his long solo number, "Why I Sing the Blues," he really soars through some heartfelt lyrics about his "frail and sickly childhood" and "those painfully introverted public-school years." The song is a triumph of melody and phrasing, and it provides some fascinating insights into the personality of this complex vocalist and biographer.

Much of the credit for the album's brilliance must go to G. E. Moore, who wrote "Principia Ethica," the group's biggest hit, as well as to Lady Ottoline Morrell, their sound technician and roadie. The efforts of professionals like these, combined with Bloomsbury's natural dynamism, have produced that rarest of rarities—a live album that is every bit as good as being there.

II

SAILCAT TURNER REMINISCES ABOUT THE
FOUNDING OF THE BLOOMSBURY GROUP

People will tell you nowadays, "Well, the Bloomsbury Group this or the Bloomsbury Group that," or "Bertrand Russell and Sir Kenneth Clark were members of the original Bloomsbury Group," or some such jive misinformation. I don't pay 'em no mind. Because, dig, I knew the Bloomsbury Group before there ever *was* a Bloomsbury Group, before anybody knew there was going to *be* any Bloomsbury Group, and I was in on the very beginning.

One night in '39, I was playing alto with McShann's band uptown at the old Savoy Ballroom—mostly blues, 'cause we had one of the better blues shouters of the day, Walter Brown—and Dizzy Gillespie was sittin' out front. So after the set Diz comes up to me and he says, "Sailcat, I got this chick that you just *got* to hear. Man, this chick can *whale.*" So he takes me over to Dan Wall's Chili Joint on Seventh Avenue, and in the back there they got a small combo—two horns, some skins, and a buddy of mine named Biddy Fleet on guitar. They're just runnin' some new chords when from this table near the stage this chick steps up. She's got what you might call a distracted air. She looks around the room nervous-like, and then she throws back her head and sound comes out like no sound I ever heard before. Man, I sat there till eight o'clock in the morning, listening to her. I asked Diz who this

5

chick was, and he says, "Don't you know? That's little Ginny Stephen." Now, of course, everybody talks about Virginia Woolf, author of *To the Lighthouse*, and so on. When I first knew her, she was just little Ginny Stephen. But man, that chick could *whale*.

I liked her music so much that me and Diz and Billie Holiday and Ginny and Ginny's sister Vanessa started hanging out together. So one day Ginny says to me, "Sailcat, I got this economist friend of mine, he's really outta sight. Would you like to meet him?" So I said sure, and she took me downtown to the Village Vanguard, and that was the first time I ever heard John Maynard Keynes. Of course, his playing wasn't much back then. Truth is, he shouldn't have been on the stage at all. Back then he was doin' "What Becomes of the Broken Hearted," but it sure didn't sound like the hit he later made it into. Back then he was still doin' "What Becomes of the Broken Hearted" as a *demonstration*, with charts and bar graphs. Later, of course, he really started cookin' and smokin'. That cat took classical economic theory and bent it in directions nobody ever thought it could go.

Now, Ginny and John, they were pretty tight, and they had this other friend they used to run with. This was a dude named Lytton Strachey, that later became their lead singer. He also won a wide reputation as an author and a critic. After hours, they used to sit around and jam and trade aphorisms. Me and Cootie Williams and Duncan Grant and Billie Holiday and Leonard Woolf, who later married Ginny, and Ella Fitzgerald, who had just taken over Chick Webb's band, and James (Lytton's brother) and Dizzy and the Duke and Maynard Keynes and Satchmo and Charles

Mingus and Theodore Llewelyn Davies and Theloni-
ous Monk and Charles Tennyson and Miles Davis and
Ray Charles and Hilton Young (later Lord Kennet) all
used to sit in sometimes too. We smoked some reefer.
Man, we used to *cook.*

Well, that was the beginning. Later, a lot of people
dropped out, and Lytton and Ginny and Vanessa and
Maynard and Leonard and Duncan and some of the
others started to call themselves the Bloomsbury
Group, after their old high school over in England.
They asked me and Diz to join, but Diz was supposed
to go on tour with Billy Eckstine's band, and as for me,
well, I wasn't too crazy about the group's strong Hel-
lenic leanings. Now, of course, I wish I'd said yes.

III
VIRGINIA WOOLF TALKS FRANKLY
ABOUT THE BLOOMSBURY GROUP

Being a member of the Bloomsbury Group has
brought me out of myself and taught me how to open
up to other people. At the beginning, all of us—Leonard, Clive, Vanessa, Lytton, Duncan, Maynard, and me
—we were like different states of mind in one con-
sciousness. It was like we each had one tarot card but
it didn't make sense until we put all the cards together,
and then when we did—it was beautiful. Like in *2001,*
when that monkey figures out how to use that bone.
Everything was merged.

Of course, we still have our problems. The interper-
sonal vibes can get pretty intense when we're touring,
going from one Quality Court to another and then to
another and then another. Sometimes I wonder if I
have room to grow as an artist. But usually it works out

7

O.K. Like the time I told Lytton that our new reggae number "Mrs. Dalloway" might work better as a short story or even a novel. We talked it out, and Lytton told me I was thinking too linear. Later, I had to admit he was right.

The hardest thing about being a member of the Bloomsbury Group is learning how to be a person at the same time you're being a star. You've got to rise above your myth. We've reached the point where we're completely supportive of each other, and that's good. But at the same time we all have our own separate lives. I've been getting into video, Maynard recorded that album with Barry White, Duncan's been doing some painting—we have to work hard to keep in touch with each other and ourselves, but it's worth it. The way I figure it, there's really nothing else I'd rather do.

KIMBERLEY SOLZHENITSYN'S CALENDAR

Two years have passed since the Russian novelist and
Nobel Prize winner Alexander Solzhenitsyn left the
Soviet Union to take up residence in the West.

—News item

May 1—Derby Day buffet at George and Dottie Balan-
chine's. Bring cranberry ketchup for the ham.

May 2—Twins to band camp. Drinks with André and
Nan Malraux.

May 8—Welcome Wagon visit in a.m. Remind Al to
drain dehumidifier pan again.

May 9—Sunday dinner at the Lévi-Strausses'. (Claude
and JoAnn. Children: Sean, 7, and I think Jason, about
4.) 1003 Red Fox Trail, Walden Estates.

May 10—Pick up twins at band camp. Take Al's old
Siberia clothes to Fire Dept. Rummage Sale.

May 11—Crêpes Club here: Mimi Sartre, Megs

Ionesco, Barb Dubuffet, Wendy Szent-Györgyi, Tracy Robbe-Grillet, Gail Miró.

May 12—Remind Al—bring patio trays up from basement. Nobel Prize winners' Spaghetti Dinner. Get Al's marimba fixed.

May 15—Al's Rotary Meeting: Brown Derby. 8:00 p.m.: To P.T.A. Mummers' *Barefoot in the Park* with Mikhail & Candy Baryshnikov.

May 17—Ecology Day. Al's old *Cancer Ward* notes to recycling center. Twins' swimming lesson—2:30: Leisure Time Pool.

May 20—Leave Subaru at the shop: oil & lube. Twins to the Balanchines'. Sam & Patsy Beckett for lunch and paddle tennis.

May 21—Hog roast at the Lévi-Strausses'.

May 24—Get twins' band uniforms cleaned for Memorial Day Parade. Al's slide show at Church Guild— "Russia: Land of Contrasts."

May 26—Blocked Writers' Benefit Car-Wash & White Sale: Church parking lot, 9:00 a.m. Evening: Gals' poker night at Cindy Böll's.

May 31—Memorial Day Horse Show: 2:00 p.m. Bring covered dish.

APARTMENT 6-A:
AFTER THE FALL

It has been over a year now since, in the wake of demoralizing setbacks, I finally abandoned my West Village apartment to the North Vietnamese. It was a time of great chaos. In my haste I had no choice but to leave behind hundreds of dollars' worth of appliances, clothing, and plants. The panic, the loss of my security deposit, getting my phone turned off, packing my small traveling bag, grabbing a taxi—all that seems like a dim nightmare to me now. But as the painful memories have lost some of their sharpness, my curiosity has grown. How has my apartment changed in the past year and a half? What have the Communists managed to make of the place where I sustained a free and democratic life for the better part of two years? I, of course, have not been allowed to visit my old piedà-terre, but from accounts of Taiwanese businessmen and Belgian journalists who have been allowed in I have managed to piece together a picture of the new Apartment 6-A at 226 Waverly Place.

More than a year after its fall, 6-A appears to be an apartment still in transition. In the living room, the Communists have retained much of my furniture, including my stereo and my portable color-TV. All the furniture and appliances that used to belong to me have been registered and given identity cards. My two end tables have been removed, under the Communists' Return to Deco Shop of Origin program. My terra-cotta fish poacher and horseshoe-crab-shell lamps have been relocated out into the country. My couch has submitted to voluntary reupholstering. The Communists have kept all my record albums, and I am told that they play them a lot. My cat, Bill, who likes to watch pigeons, seems perfectly happy with his new name, Ho Chi Minh Domestic Animal. My clippings of "Ziggy" and "Today's Chuckle" are no longer taped to the refrigerator, and in their place are Communist maxims: "Advance in the Flush of Victory with New Vigor and Remember to Get an Extra Set of Keys Made!," "Strive Resolutely to Pick Up the People's Laundry before Five!," and "Work for a Striking Development of Our Sunny Breakfast Nook!" In general, the kitchen has a more functional, lived-in look than before, when I mainly used it to prepare cans of Campbell's Chunky Beef Soup.

Among the more important dynamics at work in the redesign of my apartment is a division between two schools of thought in the Politburo of the Workers' Party. One school, the moderates, maintains that illit-

erate peasants who have only recently emerged from
the jungles and paddies after a twenty-year period of
war and apartment-hunting cannot be expected to
have any sense of design, style, color, or fabric, and
that the new government should not be afraid to hire
interior decorators who may be foreign-born or who
even may not hold to the strict Communist Party line.
The hard-liners, on the other hand, believe that coming up with a decorating scheme is well within the
powers of the North Vietnamese Army, and that all
they really have to do is put a couple of coats of barn-
red deck paint on the floor, paint the walls and ceiling
off-white, buy a couple of nice rugs and some hanging
plants and some big pillows, and then get a wheel of
Brie and throw a party to break the place in. A similar
theoretical split exists among the members of the
Phong-trao Phu-nu Giai-phong, or Freed Women
Movement, whose efforts to fix the bathroom so that
the cold-water pipe under the sink doesn't leak on the
physical therapist in 5-A have been beset with problems. The moderates advocate trying Liquid-plumr or
an Epoxi-Patch, while the hard-liners believe it is the
landlord's problem, and if he doesn't do something
about it pretty soon they favor going after the windshield of his Mercury Montego with a Volkswagen
jack. At present, the moderates hold sway in most
areas of the renovation of Apartment 6-A, and the
success of their efforts over the next few months will
very likely determine whether they or the hard-liners
will continue to formulate apartment policy in such
unresolved areas as the potentially divisive matchstick
versus traditional-plastic-venetian window-blind issue.

In recent months, the Communists have been entertaining more—having more people over at Plenteous Rice Harvest Brunches and Revere Progressive Elders At-Homes, and guests have remarked that they notice a new atmosphere of hope in my former residence. After all, it's in a nice neighborhood, and it's convenient—right on the IRT—and there are lots of things to do in the area, and the Communists have my list of sitters. They have a two-year lease on the place, so unless rent control is repealed the rent won't go up right away, and they also have a sublet clause, just in case they ever want to move on. It's a fairly safe part of town, and just a couple of blocks away there's a delicatessen that's open until two, where they sell Pepperidge Farm cookies, and there are some terrific new courses they can take at The New School, and things just might turn out to be not all that bad.

A GOOD EXPLANATION

*(A Con Ed Customer's Account of
Why the Lights Went Out)*

8:37 p.m. All is quiet at Indian Point No. 3 power station, when suddenly a huge dog jumps out of the bushes and eats several of the parts vital to the operation of the plant's main generator. As quickly as he has come, the dog disappears.

8:56 p.m. Ten miles away, at the Millwood power station, another huge dog, not the same as the first dog but a different one, jumps out of the nearby woods and eats some insulation off an important transformer. This triggers circuit breakers.

8:57 p.m. Every person in Queens between the ages of fourteen and thirty-six gets out of the shower and turns on a blow-dryer. This places an enormous strain on the power reserves of the system.

15

9:06 p.m. A guy, I don't even remember his name, nobody had ever seen him before or recognized him at all, happens to fly his helicopter over Con Edison's computerized control center on the West Side and throws a cigarette butt out the window of his helicopter, and in a one-in-a-million chance an ash lands on some computer tape and burns some holes that spell out "Shut down all systems" in computer language.

9:10 p.m. While technicians work frantically to fix the computer, yet a third huge dog attacks the power lines between Westchester and Manhattan, eating the insulators off the towers and triggering circuit breakers.

9:14 p.m. Further strain is placed on an already stretched-to-the-limits situation when every Cuisinart in Westchester turns itself on simultaneously, as if following some eerie brand-specific command.

9:17 p.m. Con Ed repairmen have just about fixed one power station when suddenly, out of the sewers—hundreds of giant white alligators! (There really is such a thing, and if you don't believe me you can call the Department of Sanitation and ask them whether there is such a thing or not.) The repairmen have to go back into their trucks and wait for the alligators to go away, and this costs precious minutes as station after station loses power.

9:19 p.m. One of Con Ed's chief engineers, working desperately against the clock, devises a plan to forestall blackout by "load shedding"—i.e., allowing power loss in some areas until the system regains its balance—and he gives the plan to Con Ed chairman Charles Luce. Before Luce can put the plan into effect,

16

however, while he is giving the first instructions by phone, he accidentally leaves the plan where his baby sister can reach it, and she gets into it and scatters the papers around and crumples up some pages and gets her teething cracker all over it. By the time he can get the papers away from her and copy them over, the domino-like sequence of power-plant shutdown is well on its way.

9:20 p.m. Throughout the five boroughs, packs of huge dogs begin eating the actual power lines.

9:30 p.m. Herds of buffalo, nobody has any idea where they came from, probably from Canada, begin stampeding across New York State and start rubbing up against the exposed power lines where the dogs have eaten off the insulation. Also, walking catfish and poisonous Mexican spitting mice do this. They impede last-minute efforts to restore power.

9:34 p.m. Total blackout.

THE END OF
BOB'S BOB HOUSE

In the thirties, it was in the basement of the old Van-
derbob Towers Hotel. In the forties, it moved into the
first floor of the Youbob Building on Fifty-second
Street. In the late fifties, it settled in what was to become its final home, the plush revolving lounge on the
top of the BobCo Building. No matter where they
found it through the years, patrons of Bob's Bob
House (and there were many who were much more
than patrons—devotees might be a better word) knew
that anyplace old Bob Bobson, God love him, was
hanging out there was sure to be excitement, fun, and
big thick steaks nearby. I'll never forget back in '54, I'd
just been fired by Bill Veeck for alcoholism, and I
walked into the Bob House with a face about a mile
long. Bob took one look at me and hollered, "Christ,

you're *sober,* Doc!" (He always called me Doc. Of course, I didn't have a medical degree, but I did have my own stapling gun. He called me Doc ever since the war, over in Korea.) "Anything you want, it's on me." My God, I drank the place dry that night, and then I had a good solid piece of American grain-fed beef and got in my car and ran over a claims adjuster and ended up in Matteawan State Hospital for the Criminally Insane. That's the kind of guy Bob was.

If you were a friend of Bob's, there was nothing he wouldn't do for you, even to the point of making soup out of your underwear and drinking the broth, as he once did for longtime crony and companion Maria Montessori, the Italian educator. But if you fell among the unfortunate few who Bob considered enemies, then look out: he might refuse to give you a good table or, looking serious, say he was going to put your dog through the bologna slicer. I'll never forget, it was June of '58 and my first ex-wife had just won a thousand dollars a month alimony so she could go and shack up with that big Mennonite buck she used to run with, plus custody of my little son and daughter. I told the judge, "God damn it, she's got the boy sleeping in a basket of fish heads—now, I don't think that's right. She's making my daughter lick dead bugs off the car radiator grille. You think that's the behavior of a fit mother?" Well, hell, she got custody anyway. The judge gave her custody. I suppose he knows better than me.

The only friend I had left in the world in those days was old Bob. I spent most of my time at the Bob House. "Mother of God, Highpockets," he'd say. (Always called me Highpockets. Course, I was only five-

eight, but I did have my own cattle prod.) "Highpockets, buddy, let me tell you what happened to my lug-
gage"—and off he'd go on a long involved rigamarole
that never failed to make me feel white again.

It was through Bob, of course, that I first met Senator
Robert Mebob. This was back before all the contro-
versy surrounding the Committee to Re-Bob Mebob,
as we all called it, which Bob got tangled up in with
that crazy prank where he and someone on the Senator's staff put a Saltine in a cup of warm tea (an allega-
tion that was never proved, by the way). At any rate,
Bob took me over to the Senator's table at the Bob
House one night. "Curly," he said to me. (He always
called me Curly. Course, I didn't have any hair of my
own, but I did have my own meat thermometer.)
"Curly," he says, "I want you to meet the Honorable
Robert Youbob Mebob—I call him Bob, buddy of
mine—he's the greatest guy, he's a helluva guy. God,
I love him. I'll bet you didn't know that this guy right
here, Senator Bob Mebob, he's the father of my oldest
boy, Bobby." Then he grinned and grabbed the Senator in a big bear hug and his eyes filled with tears, and
I have to admit I was surprised, even though I knew
that Bob's wife, who used to wait tables at the Bob
House, was a great and beautiful lady and a fine help-
meet and a terrific gal who shacked up with any
damned guy she felt like, and a terrific mother who
loved to drink and drive. Later, when the Senator got
indicted, Bob never forgot him, and once sent him five
dozen red roses with a note asking if he was still in love
with Otis Sistrunk, of the Oakland Raiders. That's
the way it was if you were friends with Bob—you

were in love with Otis Sistrunk, although probably you weren't.

Now, after forty years and who knows how many stomachs pumped, they're closing down the old Bob House, where so many of us had such great times and blacked out so many times over the years, and we're sure going to miss it. Of course, Bob has slowed down a lot, and he can't threaten people as well as he used to when he was younger, and that, along with the incident last fall where a bunch of kids broke in after hours and taped live ferrets to the salad bar, has taken a lot of the fun out of the Bob House for him. Bob is moving to Jersey, where he plans to just take it easy and collect moving violations and rifle the desks of guys who know him and trust him, and we wish him the best. I know I speak for everybody else who has known Bob and his Bob House when I say that we love him and think he's the greatest guy and the cutest guy and has done a terrific job not only for the restaurant business but also for the city as a whole.

THE SANDY FRAZIER DREAM TEAM

OFFENSE

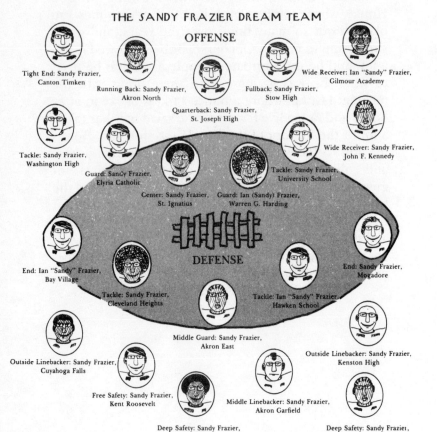

Tight End: Sandy Frazier,
Canton Timken

Running Back: Sandy Frazier,
Akron North

Quarterback: Sandy Frazier,
St. Joseph High

Fullback: Sandy Frazier,
Stow High

Wide Receiver: Ian "Sandy" Frazier,
Gilmour Academy

Tackle: Sandy Frazier,
Washington High

Guard: Sandy Frazier,
Elyria Catholic

Center: Sandy Frazier,
St. Ignatius

Guard: Ian (Sandy) Frazier,
Warren G. Harding

Tackle: Sandy Frazier,
University School

Wide Receiver: Sandy Frazier,
John F. Kennedy

DEFENSE

End: Ian "Sandy" Frazier,
Bay Village

Tackle: Sandy Frazier,
Cleveland Heights

Tackle: Ian "Sandy" Frazier,
Hawken School

End: Sandy Frazier,
Mogadore

Middle Guard: Sandy Frazier,
Akron East

Outside Linebacker: Sandy Frazier,
Cuyahoga Falls

Free Safety: Sandy Frazier,
Kent Roosevelt

Middle Linebacker: Sandy Frazier,
Akron Garfield

Outside Linebacker: Sandy Frazier,
Kenston High

Deep Safety: Sandy Frazier,
Glenville

Deep Safety: Sandy Frazier,
John Adams

THE SANDY FRAZIER DREAM TEAM

Quarterback: 6'4", 185-lb. senior Sandy Frazier led St. Joe's Vikings to their second straight all-city championship, amassing 1,593 yards in the air with an 87% completion ratio. Set state mark for rushing by a quarterback with 830 yards for the season.

Fullback: Stow junior Sandy Frazier (6'5", 217 lbs.) broke all rushing records set at Stow in 1962 by star alum Larry Csonka. Frazier is tremendously quick for a big man.

Running Back: Suspended early in the season for disciplinary reasons, Akron North's Sandy Frazier came back in the final three games to beat Hoban, Buchtel, and Firestone with his spectacular catches and kickoff returns. He runs the hundred in 9.4, an excellent time for a man his size.

Wide Receiver: Sandy Frazier of John F. Kennedy caught 45 passes for touchdowns this season. Team captain in his sophomore year, he will make the Fighting Eagles squad of 17 returning lettermen a power in the '78 city championships.

Wide Receiver: The Lancers cruised to the Greater Cleveland Private School title behind the receiving and open-field blocking of 6'5", 195-lb. junior end Ian "Sandy" Frazier. For a man of his size, he possesses outstanding quickness and agility.

Tight End: Canton Timken relied on their big junior tight end Sandy Frazier for his blocking on traps and sweeps, as well as for his pass-catching abilities. His quickness is amazing, considering his height and weight (6'7", 223 lbs.).

Tackle: Massillon's Washington High has produced more pro tackles than any other high school in the country, and 6'8", 260-lb. junior Sandy Frazier is well on his way to joining that list. He moves with great agility for a tackle that large.

Tackle: University School's four-year letterman and team captain Sandy Frazier displays surprising quickness, despite his 6'2", 230-lb. frame.

Guard: Ian (Sandy) Frazier of Warren G. Harding really made the Panthers' ground game roll. The 6'3", 215-lb. senior is an excellent pulling guard, with his 9.8 speed.

Guard: Elyria Catholic senior Sandy Frazier, at 6'4" and 240 lbs., is a lineman who can do it all. He has great mobility for a big man.

Center: St. Ignatius sophomore Sandy Frazier, at 5'11", 212 lbs., was the dependable keystone of the Maize and Blue offense this year, which ranked third in total yardage in the state prep totals.

DEFENSE

Deep Safety: John Adams coach Paul Feldermacher calls 5'9", 165-lb. junior defensive back Sandy Frazier "pound for pound the best player I have ever coached." He wins the Dream-Team Headhunter Award for most tackles this season.

Deep Safety: 5'11", 175-lb. senior Sandy Frazier of Glenville won the East Cleveland Thanksgiving Turkey Day Game with his 85-yard runback of an interception in the final seconds.

Free Safety: A player skilled at reading defenses who also loves to hit people, Kent Roosevelt junior Sandy Frazier was the headache of running backs throughout the greater Akron area, with his 6'7", 210-lb. build coupled with his excellent speed.

Outside Linebacker: Sandy Frazier of Cuyahoga Falls, a 6'3", 210-lb. junior, led the Suburban League in tackles per game. He is as fast and nimble as a man half his size.

Outside Linebacker: Kenston High's junior defender Sandy Frazier (6'4", 215 lbs.) played with reckless abandon in the Class AA Divisional Championship, blocking three punts. Even though he is huge, he is also swift.

Middle Linebacker: A narrow choice in the Dream Team voting over Walsh Jesuit's outstanding MLB Sandy Frazier, Akron Garfield senior captain Sandy

Frazier won out because even though he clocks a speedy 4.2 in the 40-yard dash, he is still extremely large (6′2″, 210 lbs.).

End: Bay Village High senior DE Ian "Sandy" Frazier, at 6′6″, 231 lbs., has the catlike quickness which makes him a really tough defender, when you consider how big he is.

End: Mogadore owes most of its 6–3 won-lost record to sophomore defensive end Sandy Frazier, who intimidated blockers with his agility, which was outstanding when operating in concert with his 6′5″, 223-lb. body.

Tackle: Ian "Sandy" Frazier of Hawken School is a player who you would think would move slow off the ball when you realized that he weighs in at 6′8″, 240 lbs., but that was not the case, as many prep-league opponents can attest.

Tackle: Cleveland Heights junior standout Sandy Frazier (6′3″, 219 lbs.) made game-saving tackles three times in goal-line stands when the Heights Tigers shut out the mighty Blue Bombers of Cleveland East. He is very large, in addition to being very fast.

Middle Guard: Akron East junior Sandy Frazier was the mainstay of East's defense, which allowed only 24 points all season. For a man of his quickness and agility, he possesses tremendous size.

DATING YOUR MOM

In today's fast-moving, transient, rootless society, where people meet and make love and part without ever really touching, the relationship every guy already has with his own mother is too valuable to ignore. Here is a grown, experienced, loving woman— one you do not have to go to a party or a singles bar to meet, one you do not have to go to great lengths to get to know. There are hundreds of times when you and your mother are thrown together naturally, without the tension that usually accompanies courtship— just the two of you, alone. All you need is a little presence of mind to take advantage of these situations. Say your mom is driving you downtown in the car to buy you a new pair of slacks. First, find a nice station on the car radio, one that she likes. Get into the

pleasant lull of freeway driving—tires humming along
the pavement, air-conditioner on max. Then turn to
look at her across the front seat and say something
like, "You know, you've really kept your shape, Mom,
and don't think I haven't noticed." Or suppose she
comes into your room to bring you some clean socks.
Take her by the wrist, pull her close, and say, "Mom,
you're the most fascinating woman I've ever met."
Probably she'll tell you to cut out the foolishness, but
I can guarantee you one thing: she will never tell your
dad. Possibly she would find it hard to say, "Dear,
Piper just made a pass at me," or possibly she is se-
cretly flattered, but, whatever the reason, she will keep
it to herself until the day comes when she is no longer
ashamed to tell the world of your love.

Dating your mother seriously might seem difficult at
first, but once you try it I'll bet you'll be surprised at
how easy it is. Facing up to your intention is the main
thing: you have to want it bad enough. One problem
is that lots of people get hung up on feelings of guilt
about their dad. They think, Oh, here's this kindly old
guy who taught me how to hunt and whittle and dyna-
mite fish—I can't let him go on into his twilight years
alone. Well, there are two reasons you can dismiss
those thoughts from your mind. First, *every* woman, I
don't care who she is, prefers her son to her husband.
That is a simple fact; ask any woman who has a son,
and she'll admit it. And why shouldn't she prefer
someone who is so much like herself, who represents
nine months of special concern and love and intense
physical closeness—someone whom she actually
created? As more women begin to express the need to
have something all their own in the world, more

women are going to start being honest about this preference. When you and your mom begin going together, you will simply become part of a natural and inevitable historical trend.

Second, you must remember this about your dad: you have your mother, he has his! Let him go put the moves on his own mother and stop messing with yours. If his mother is dead or too old to be much fun anymore, that's not your fault, is it? It's not your fault that he didn't realize his mom for the woman she was, before it was too late. Probably he's going to try a lot of emotional blackmail on you just because you had a good idea and he never did. Don't buy it. Comfort yourself with the thought that your dad belongs to the last generation of guys who will let their moms slip away from them like that.

Once your dad is out of the picture—once he has taken up fly-tying, joined the Single Again Club, moved to Russia, whatever—and your mom has been wooed and won, if you're anything like me you're going to start having so much fun that the good times you had with your mother when you were little will seem tame by comparison. For a while, Mom and I went along living a contented, quiet life, just happy to be with each other. But after several months we started getting into some different things, like the big motorized stroller. The thrill I felt the first time Mom steered me down the street! On the tray, in addition to my Big Jim doll and the wire with the colored wooden beads, I have my desk blotter, my typewriter, an in-out basket, and my name plate. I get a lot of work done, plus I get a great chance to people-watch. Then there's my big, adult-sized highchair, where I sit in the evening as Mom and I watch the news and discuss current events, while I paddle in my food and throw my dishes on the floor. When Mom reaches to wipe off my chin and I take her hand, and we fall to the floor in a heap—me, Mom, highchair, and all—well, those are the best times, those are the very best times.

It is true that occasionally I find myself longing for even more—for things I know I cannot have, like the feel of a firm, strong, gentle hand at the small of my back lifting me out of bed into the air, or someone who could walk me around and burp me after I've watched all the bowl games and had about nine beers. Ideally, I would like a mom about nineteen or twenty feet tall, and although I considered for a while asking my mom to start working out with weights and drinking Nutrament, I finally figured, Why put her through it? After all, she is not only my woman, she is my best friend. I have to take her as she is, and the way she is is plenty good enough for me.

NIVEN:
A RECONSIDERATION

Over the years, it has been the custom of literary critics to regard Niven as a lonely monument, self-created —almost as much a fiction as one of his own characters, magnificent in the uniqueness of his achievement. While I realize that this is doctrine from which one of our number strays at his peril, I have always believed that such a view of the man and his work removes Niven from his historical context and neglects consideration of the author as a product of the turbulent intellectual climate of his time. One must remember that it was during Niven's age that Hope also wrote. Although Hope had produced most of his œuvre (including the major works, *Have Tux, Will Travel, So This Is Peace,* and his masterpiece, *I Owe Russia $1,200*) a number of years before Niven wrote

The Moon's a Balloon, he was still alive in the full noon of Niven's day, and they may even have known each other. We should remember, too, that it was about this time that MacLaine produced her *Don't Fall Off the Mountain,* Arnaz his *A Book,* and Boone his *Twixt Twelve and Twenty.* And what of Davis, Jr.? His *Yes I Can,* which predates Niven's *Balloon,* has a clean, architectonic style reminiscent of Nivenian prose. Indeed, is it mere coincidence that Davis, Jr.'s work even contains some of the same characters that we find in both *Balloon* and *Bring on the Empty Horses?*

The only author to whom critics might concede some legitimate claim to Niven's spiritual paternity is Sam Levenson, and even here I feel they have always missed an important point; namely, that the title of one of Levenson's finest works, *In One Era and Out the Other,* with its punning play on the word "era" (and its nicely coupled sense of words going in one *ear* and out the other, from the popular expression, much as ideas that are "in" to members of one generation, or era, may be "out"—i.e., not only unfashionable but also out of mind—to the members of another) may well have provided Niven with the inspiration for similar assonantal play with whimsy and daring internal rhyme in the brilliant title of his first masterpiece.

It is unfortunate that critics have all too often lost sight of the fact that David Niven's works are, above all, stories, full of fun and adventure, depicted by an artist who knew enough not to spare the bold strokes. I wonder how many scholars lost in Nivenolatry can remember their joy at first meeting the roistering Errol Flynn, the puckish David Selznick, or the magisterial Louis B. Mayer. I sometimes wish that I could will myself into forgetting his marvelous scene with Mrs. Nikita Khrushchev and Frank Sinatra at the welcoming banquet, so that I could once more taste the delight of reading it for the first time.

Niven experiences life as an imprisoning reality of personal experience, plus mythopoeic elements, a vast *sottisier* in the tradition of Jessel's *This Way, Miss.* In a time when many writers have designs on recondite allusions, his works are a valued presence. Behind the intelligence, etc., is an attitude best summarized.

HOW I DID IT

I knew first that you have to have faith you're going to get the cards when you aren't getting the cards, and second that when you do get the cards you have to *bet it up.* Plus I figured it works for him, it'll work for you, so I just went out and copied him, got the exact same technique, the exact same timing—everything. I practically traced him. This wouldn't have worked any other day, either, wouldn't have worked any other time, but you know the way the road gets kind of wide there by Herrick Park where they made the turnaround for the road-grading equipment—well, I figured that at this time of day, with the tide being twenty minutes later on the Gulf side, there would still be just enough water to float us over but not enough for those big federal boats, and with the sun just hit-

34

ting the horizon they're going to have the light right in their eyes when we go over. They had signals that they shouted, and suddenly I realized after I'd heard it for the fourth time that they were calling an audible, where Bev and Marsha aren't both going to be able to ride home with Roy and you remember how much Marsha has always wanted to go to the Tennessee Tap but Roy would never let her, so I said, "I've got to stop to the Tap for a minute but then I'll run you on home," and of course she bit. Another thing that didn't hurt at all was the fact that a lot of these people came from really poor backgrounds and didn't have even one-tenth the advantages I had—their mothers feeding them Nugrape instead of formula and vitamins and not knowing anything about nutrition probably knocked their college-board scores down a hundred points right there. So that made it easy—all I had to do was copy it all down on my ankle and then razor the chapter out of every book in the library. It was beautiful. It was really beautiful. I noticed that the birds always seemed to go up right after we'd broken our guns to climb a fence, so when we got to a part of the field where it looked good I broke my gun without ejecting the shell and then closed it quietly and stood there ready, and sure enough after about fifteen seconds I'm positive she's going to walk away without saying anything but then she turns to me and looks at me for a long time and then she hands me a paper plate with her telephone number written on it. Luckily, when I took my license out of my breast pocket the highway patrolman wasn't looking and I was able to palm the cannister and instead of trying to chuck it away I just held it in my hand and although they

35

searched everywhere I knew the man was a new man and he still wasn't comfortable acting so hard and letting his position keep him from everybody else so I offered him a piece of chewing gum and we got to talking and suddenly I realized that their entire left flank was up in the air! It wasn't up against a mountain or river or anything and there was no cavalry to protect it so I went out and bought an entire new suit and a new pair of shoes and got a fake ID made up and then all I needed was an official insignia for the ID and then it came to me: a model-car kit would have decals in it about the right size so I bought one and it fit perfectly and as I was standing there I said to myself, "Oh, God, they know I'm lying, they know I'm a fake," and then the lady comes up to me and says, "Your table is ready now, Mr. Selznick," and I felt so great. The grayout from the force of the Gs began to fade and my vision returned and I saw maybe four thousand feet below me two of the A-37 strike force that had come out with us barreling along back to the base with their afterburners going and then it hit me —*A-37s don't have afterburners!* And that's when I realized that they were MIGs, so I walked over to them and said, "Miss—or Mrs., as the case may be—would you care to dance with me?" and that was when I knew that I totally had them.

INTO THE
AMERICAN MAW

I was driving back to New York from Boston last Sunday and I stopped in a restaurant to get something to eat, and as I sat there waiting for my order to come, looking at my ice water and my silverware and the paper placemat, suddenly something struck me: I just might be on a savage nightmare journey to the heart of the American dream! I wasn't sure exactly what savage nightmare journeys to the heart of the American dream required, but I knew that since America has a love affair with the automobile, it was probably difficult to pursue a nightmare journey on public transportation. Fortunately, I had my own car, a 1970 Maverick. Beyond that, I couldn't think of any hard-and-fast requirements, so I decided that I *was* on a savage journey to the heart of the American dream, and I was glad that it was a Sunday. That made it more convenient for me. Once I had accepted this possibility, it was amazing how I saw all of America in a new light. Insights started coming to me one after the other, and I decided to reveal them in a voice as flat and affectless as the landscape that surrounded me (I was in a relatively flat part of Connecticut at the time).

First, I realized that discount stores—you know, the discount stores you see all over the place in America —well, I realized that discount stores equal emptiness. Beyond that, I realized that different discount stores represent different shades of emptiness—Caldor's equals an emptiness tinged with a sad, ineffable sense of mourning for a lost American innocence, while Brands Mart equals an emptiness much closer to what European philosophers call "anomie," and Zayre's equals an emptiness along the lines of Sartre's "nausea." Next, I realized that the interstate highway system equals nihilism. Have you ever been on Interstate 75 north of Berea, Kentucky? If you have, you know the stretch I'm thinking of—it's one of the most nihilistic stretches of four-lane possibly in the whole world. Although there certainly are lots of nihilistic interstate highways in every state in this country. In California, every stretch of road—I don't care whether it's interstate or a state highway or a county road or gravel or asphalt or oil—all of it is nihilistic.

Thinking about California led me to dizzying thoughts about L.A.—L.A., where sometimes on the signs advertising used-car lots they actually spell "car" with a "k." . . . L.A., a place that is so different from the East Coast. New York City, of course, is a woman. In fact, the entire tristate area, including New York,

Connecticut, and New Jersey, is a woman. But L.A.—
L.A. is the City of the One-Night Stands. Or at least
that's what I had heard. Just to be sure, I decided to
call L.A. long-distance, my voice crying through wires
across the vast, buffalo-scarred dreamscape of a
haunted republic. I told L.A. that I was coming out for
four days, and could I possibly get a three-night stand.
They said no, sir. They said I had to get three one-
night stands. Q.E.D.

I paid my check and left the restaurant and got in my
car. Luckily, it started. I began to drive—to drive to
nowhere on a vast blank ribbon, to drive without direction or purpose (beyond getting home sometime
that evening), surrounded by other Americans, my
partners in the dream, all of them sealed off from me
and each other by metal and glass. It got dark and
began to rain, and still I was driving. I turned on the
windshield wipers, and it wasn't long before I saw in
the windshield the images of all my fathers before me.
I saw my great-great-grandfathers' faces—not all eight
of my great-great-grandfathers' faces but, say, maybe
five of them—and then I saw my great-grandfathers
and my grandfathers and my father, and all the faces
merged into my face, reflected in the blue light from
the dashboard as the wipers swished back and forth.
And then my face changed into the faces of people
who I guess were supposed to be my descendants.
And still I was driving, stopping only occasionally to
pay either thirty cents or twenty-five cents for tolls. I
was on that stretch of 95 where you have to pay tolls
every ten miles or so.

I stopped at a gas station to buy cigarettes. I put
eighty cents in change into the machine, and pulled

the knob for my brand—Camel Lights. Nothing came out. Then I pulled the knob for Vantage. Nothing came out. Then I pushed the coin return, and nothing came out. Then I pulled all of the other knobs, and nothing came out—a metaphor.

LGA-ORD

Then, Beckett decided to become a commercial pilot
. . .

> "I think the next little bit of excitement is flying,"
> he wrote to McGreevy. "I hope I am not too old to take
> it up seriously nor too stupid about machines to qual-
> ify as a commercial pilot."
> —*Samuel Beckett: A Biography,* by Deirdre Bair

Gray bleak final afternoon ladies and gentlemen this is your captain your cap welcoming you aboard the continuation of Flyways flight 185 from nothingness to New York's Laguardia non non non non non non nonstop to Chicago's Ohare and on from there in the passing of gray afternoons to empty bleak eternal nothingness again with the Carey bus the credit-card machine the Friskem metal detector the boarding pass the in-flight magazine all returned to tiny bits of grit blowing across the steppe for ever
(Pause)
Cruising along nicely now.
(Pause)
Yes cruising along very nicely indeed if I do say so myself.

(Long pause)
Twenty-two thousand feet.
(Pause)
Extinguish the light extinguish the light I have extinguished the No Smoking light so you are free to move about the cabin have a good cry hang yourselves get an erection who knows however we do ask that while you're in your seats you keep your belts lightly fastened in case we encounter any choppy air or the end we've prayed for past time remembering our flying time from New York to Chicago is two hours and fifteen minutes the time of the dark journey of our existence is not revealed, you cry no you *pray* for a flight attendant you pray for a flight attendant a flight attendant comes now cry with reading material if you care to purchase a cocktail
(Pause)
A cocktail?
(Pause)
If you care to purchase a piece of carrot, a stinking turnip, a bit of grit our flight attendants will be along to see that you know how to move out of this airplane fast and use seat lower back cushion for flotation those of you on the right side of the aircraft ought to be able to see New York's Finger Lakes region that's Lake Canandaigua closest to us those of you on the left side of the aircraft will only see the vastness of eternal emptiness without end
(Pause)
(Long pause)
(Very long pause)
(Long pause of about an hour)

42

We're beginning our descent we're finished nearly
finished soon we will be finished we're beginning our
descent our long descent ahh descending beautifully
to Chicago's Ohare Airport ORD ORD ORD ORD seat
backs and tray tables in their full upright position for
landing for ending flight attendants prepare for ending it is ending the flight is ending please check the
seat pocket in front of you to see if you have all your
belongings with you remain seated and motionless
until the ending until the finish until the aircraft has
come to a complete stop at the gate until the end
(Pause)
When we deplane I'll weep for happiness.

THE MUSEUM

On cold, cold winter nights—when pitiless wolves come bounding across the frozen surface of Gunflint Lake, on the border between Minnesota and Ontario, now yipping and snarling, now calling in a high-pitched, keening wail, now silent and intent, pursuing a whitetail deer that they have startled from its bed, moving like shadows across the snow through the forests of alder and pine and white spruce and red osier dogwood in an easy lope that can carry them for miles without tiring—then is the best time to raise funds for the Pitiless Lamb-Murder Museum.

I am Sandy ffonville-Woof, the curator of the museum. My mother was a ffonville, from one of the first families of St. Paul, Minnesota, and through her

44

I trace my ancestry back to Norman nobility. My father was a huge timber wolf. (The word, by the way, is properly spelled as it should be pronounced—*woof*, with a short *oo*—and I continue to spell my name the older, more correct way, rather than accept the modern corruption, *wolf*, a word I can spell but not for the life of me pronounce.) In the winter of 1928, one of the coldest winters anyone remembers, my mother was staying at her family's cabin in Minnesota's Boundary Waters. One night, right around midnight, with curtains of Northern Lights in the background, she met a huge Eastern timber woof bounding across the frozen surface of Gunflint Lake. They fell in love, and the following June they were married in St. Andrew's Episcopal Church in St. Paul, my mother wearing a gown of cream-colored tulle trimmed with Venetian lace and holding a bouquet of black-eyed Susans and baby's breath, and my father yipping, snarling, biting, and howling a high-pitched, keening wail.

I was born a normal boy except for the woofish silver-gray hackles between my shoulder blades, and I grew up in a loving crowd of uncles, aunts, cousins, and grandparents. I had the first go-cart in the neighborhood. It was gas-powered and could go twenty-five miles an hour. One day I drove it off the track that Grandpa ffonville had built for me and onto Interstate 35, which ran near our house, and when my mother found out she sent me to bed without my supper. I lay in bed scared to death that when my father came home he would nip me about the head and shoulders with his powerful jaws, which made a sound like two pieces

45

of floorboarding being clapped together. When I heard his claws click across the tile of the family room downstairs, I crawled to the far end of the bed and hid under the covers. But when I peeked out, I saw him coming through the door at an easy canter carrying a fat yearling heifer that must have weighed almost as much as he did, full off the floor. He dropped it next to my bed, and then he showed me how to find the choicest parts—the hindquarters, the loin, and the leaf fat around the kidneys. Then we took the carcass outside and buried it in the back yard.

My mother, accustomed to the usages of St. Paul society, never really fit in with the pack of ravenous, tireless timber wooves that my father hunted with. I remember when he tried to teach her how to bobtail cattle—that is, how to chase cattle across a pasture and snip their tails off at full speed with one powerful bite. She tried and tried, but lacking two- and three-inch-long canine teeth, she never could get the hang of it. My father, for his part, did not get along well with her family, and sometimes when they came by the house he would harry them across frozen wastelands for days until they dropped from sheer exhaustion. But I believe that, deep down, my parents were devoted to each other. Wooves mate for life, and after my mother died my father never took another mate. He lost himself in his work, and became one of the last great stock-killing wooves of northern Minnesota. He eluded government trappers who came from seven states to try to end his depredations, and although no sign was seen of him in the territory after 1963, he was never captured.

•

It was through a friend of my father, Old Three Toes of Lac Qui Parle County, that I first became involved with the Pitiless Lamb-Murder Museum. I was in my early thirties at the time, working for the St. Paul Historical Society, and dissatisfied because I felt the society did not put enough emphasis on the hamstringing of sheep. Then Old Three Toes led me, with barks and whines, to a museum in the twilit north woods of Minnesota's Boundary Waters—a museum founded in 1906 by pitiless, yipping, snarling, biting, hamstringing wooves to commemorate the slaughter of helpless, fleecy-white little lambs. I realized immediately that I had found my life's work.

The Pitiless Lamb-Murder Museum sits in a broad clearing in the Northern forest of alder and pine and white spruce and red osier dogwood. In front of the museum are the bobtailing grounds, with spectator stands and stock chutes at one end, and a practice area and special tooth-sharpening rocks at the other. Behind the museum are the pens for cattle, sheep, hogs, horses, deer, caribou, elk, reindeer, big-horn rams, dall sheep, mountain goats, varying hares, marmots, ground squirrels, rabbits, lemmings, and mice. Entering the museum at an easy lope, the visitor first passes through the Outrages in Broad Daylight exhibits. There, helpless immigrants huddle on tree limbs while red wooves made bold by hunger devour their draft oxen and mules, animals that represent the immigrants' life savings. It is midday, but the wooves do not care. There, also, gunmetal-blue wooves, five feet tall at the shoulders, with bright orange teeth, follow close behind office workers on their way to their jobs in Northern cities, breathing horrible woof-breath down their necks. In another exhibit, you see first blue-eyed, fluffy white baby lambs with pink ribbons around their necks frolicking innocently around gentle, benign wooves. Next, you see the wooves' expressions change to interest. Then you see the wooves staggering meat-drunk, and nothing left of the lambs but pieces of pink ribbon in woof stool.

In the rest of the museum, it is night. In most of the exhibits, it is an arctic night, so cold that your nostril hairs freeze and break off. In one exhibit, there are no wooves, only woof howls, and two thousand frightened caribou. A pack of wooves have spread out over the caribou's night range, and a woof howls. The caribou run from him. Then the next woof howls, and the caribou run from him. Then the next woof, and the next, and so on until morning, when grinning wooves descend on the exhausted herd. Another display shows a blinding snowstorm, with huge flakes driven by a sixty-mile-an-hour wind. A herd of deer is yarding —standing close together in a small clearing in the deep woods for warmth—when suddenly out of the storm, as if they were part of the storm themselves, without warning leap pitiless Leonard Woof, Virginia Woof, and Thomas Woof, their hackles hoary with snow, cruel teeth bared, plumes of steam blowing from their flared nostrils. They bring down many more of the deer than they could possibly eat, apparently just for the fun of it!

Wooves, pitiless wooves, my ancestors, now driven to the extreme places of the continent!

Thanks should go to the National Trust for Historic Preservation and the Tandy Company for the generous grants that have enabled the museum to continue

48

its work, and that sponsored the clinics at the museum for wooves, coyotes, and coydogs. With help, the museum does what it can, remembering that nothing anyone could do today will ever bring back the age of unchecked predation by wooves.

~~~~~~

LIST OF FUNNY
NAMES RELEASED

The B. Robert Bobson Memorial Foundation has announced the winners of its fellowship grant awards for 1981–1982. Chosen from a field of more than 4,000 applicants, the 305 winners will share $8 million in award money in this the sixtieth year since the Bobson Foundation was set up "to provide financial assistance to promising artists, scholars, scientists, and shoppers."

A list of the winners in your area, along with their proposed projects:

Arthur Access, writer: a novelization.

Sean Allen, composer: a symphonization.

Patsy Angst, sculptor in residence, School of Artistic Supply: a kinetic sculpturization.

Carl Birdperson, associate professor of particle physics, Exact Change University: "If You Hit the Hope Diamond with a Sledgehammer, Would It Break?"

Bud Buh, writer: three film treatments, a TV pilot, and a couple concepts.

Seymour Butts, writer: a novel, *Under the Grandstand.*

Marc Cohen, filmmaker: being filmic.

Constance Crevecoeur, Martha Simpson Strong Professor of English Literature, Leading College: "The Novel *Finnegans Wake:* What th'-?!"

Kathy Diaghilev, choreographer: studying the dances of many lands and peoples.

John Diefenbacher, notewright: writing notes.

Perry Freud, sexologist: pure theoretical sexology.

Steve from Downstairs, artist: creating art.

Page Gauge, painter: apartments, stores, lofts, interior & exterior.

Walter Guff, professor of American-European history, Impressive Transcript University: "World War II: Nothing but a Big Media Circus."

Tom Italianfood, poet: writing something that will be so much like poetry as to be virtually indistinguishable from it.

Raymond Jackson, male, 6'2", early twenties, wearing a blue windbreaker and white tennis cap: "Give Us Your Money or We Will Cut You with a Linoleum Knife" (in collaboration with William Wilson).

Ivan Kipling, professor of the humanities, Kevin's College: "Studies in the Comparative Intelligence of Several Experts in the Politics of the Caribbean Basin and My Cat, Tibbs."

Andrea Nope, poet: a sonnetization.

Laura Orals, professor of French and chicken farming, New People College: *"A la Recherche du Frank Perdue."*

Ranch Quentin, plagiarist: copying out William Faulkner's "The Bear" word for word.

Rick Ratatouille, parasculptor: hopefully getting a chance to meet and work with some real sculptors.

Johnny So-what, poet in residence, Springfield Elementary: saying "So what" and "Oh, huh" and "I bet."

Ted Tedshack, video artist: watching whatever's on.

Rowena Utter, pretend choreographer: pretend choreography.

William Wilson, male, 5'10", early twenties, wearing a tan jacket and a Pittsburgh Pirates baseball cap: "Give Us Your Money or We Will Cut You with a Linoleum Knife" (in collaboration with Raymond Jackson).

Bob Youbob, writer: behaving in a fictive manner.

WHAT THE DOG DID

I came home the other day and my Saint Bernard, Tiffany, had a really guilty expression on her face, with her ears all hanging down. I got a hunch. I went into the living room, and there were all the cushions on the floor, and dog hairs all over the davenport. She knows she's not supposed to be up there. I said, "Come here, you!" and I whacked her with a rolled-up newspaper. She knew she had it coming. She went out in the mud room and lay down with her head right on the floor while I cleaned up the mess she'd made. Finally I figured she'd had enough, so I said, "Come on, girl, you're a good dog now." I went to give her a Liv-a-Snap, and the next thing I knew she wagged her tail so hard she knocked a full ashtray right off the kitchen table! —IAN FRAZIER

•

A NOTE ON THE AUTHOR: *Ian Frazier is a writer who soaks up experience like a sponge. He experiences life as vividly and adjectivally as he writes about it. His appetite for life is as large as the man himself, or even somewhat larger, since Ian Frazier is of average size and his appetite for life is way above average. He has been embracing all of experience since he was eleven years old, when he began riding his bike to school and so escaped the crushing, stultifying influence of his parents. He spent his pre-teen years traveling, hunting, and fishing as a protégé of novelist Ernest Hemingway, whom he later broke with when he noticed that the older writer continually addressed him as "Daughter." Now in his mid-thirties, a mature writer who has triumphantly found his own voice, he remains (paradoxically) very much a child in many ways. He has that type of courage which one finds so rarely in an adult in our society, and that is the courage to play. It's been said that the eminent student of the human mind Carl Jung abandoned his career and his responsibilities in his sixties and spent a year building sand castles on the beach; that would be as nothing to Ian Frazier. He is just constantly playing. Sometimes he'll give oranges to people on the subway. Sometimes he'll pull a chair out from under a friend when that friend is about to sit down. Sometimes he'll send people unnecessary packages Air Express, making sure that the package will arrive at an inconvenient time. He is blessed with a fractured vision, and a conviction that the world is mad. In spite of that (or perhaps because of that), he doesn't judge another fellow until he has walked around for a while in that fellow's shoes. And not just guys' shoes—sometimes he walks around in ladies' shoes, too: anklestraps, Mary Janes, high heels, flats, and sling-backs. And all the people coming around his apartment trying to get their shoes back, and the confusion, the arguments—unpleasant, perhaps, but all part of a writer's life. Any experience that happens, it doesn't just have to be a good experience, and—BAM—Ian Frazier will convert it to writing of some kind. Say he's flying from New York to Miami and his plane has a layover at a Southern airport like Atlanta. Within a matter of minutes, he'll be writing a postcard, the scent of heliotrope and verbena and honeysuckle pervading his prose, and he will be infused with a tremendous sense of place. Or, to give another example, say he's sitting around at a party and someone puts an old song on the record-player and the song reminds him of eighth grade. Suddenly it will be as if he actually is in eighth grade for a while in his mind. Then maybe he'll notice a Fedders air-conditioner in the window next to where he's sitting and he'll be reminded of a Fedders air-conditioner he owned in 1975 that broke down once in the hottest part of the summer. Then something else will bring another memory to mind and off he'll go again. He'll be in the same room with you and yet not there, all at the same time. His writing shows evidence of the strong influence of Sardou, Mazo de la Roche, and Juanita Bartlett. Some critics have called him the white Paul Laurence Dunbar. He lives in Paris, France, with eight mistresses, one of whom is a former Miss Universe runner-up. Everyone he has ever met is completely crazy about him.*

~~~~~~

THE STUTTGART FOLDERS

Martin Van Buren, eighth President of the United States, stared gloomily out of his office window.—first line of *Oregon!* by Dana Fuller Ross

The President swiveled in his chair, clasped his hands behind his head, and stared unseeing out of the window of the Oval Office and cursed his lot.—first line of *Raise the Titanic!* by Clive Cussler

He was seated in the dark, alone, behind the desk of Hajib Kafir, staring unseeingly out of the dusty office window at the timeless minarets of Istanbul.—first line of *Bloodline* by Sidney Sheldon

One year later: It was a gray, brutally cold March day in Moscow. Dmitri Chakhovsky stood before the window of his small, plainly furnished office inside KGB headquarters. He stared down to a deserted Dzerzhinsky Square, his thoughts on the approaching spring.—first lines of *The Windchime Legacy* by A. W. Mykel.

DiMona, meanwhile, has just published a novel with Morrow entitled *To the Eagle's Nest*, which he says has the most commercial opening line of any novel ever published. He may be right. The opening is "Adolf Hitler slipped off his bathrobe and stood naked."—*Washington Star*

"And what are you staring at, Herr Himmler?" Adolf Hitler asked as he strode into the high-ceilinged conference room.

"Uh, nothing, Führer," Himmler said, blushing and looking away.

"Nothing? And what about you, Herr Reichsmar-schall?" he asked, turning to Goering. "Why did your eyes practically pop out of your head?"

Goering cleared his throat as if to speak, and then just looked at the floor. There was a long pause.

Then Grand Admiral of the Navy Doenitz spoke up, in a wavering voice. "It's simply that . . . if the Führer will permit me . . . you're . . . in the altogether."

"I'm buck naked—that's what you're saying, isn't it?" Hitler asked. "Do you think I don't know that? Of course I'm *au naturel,* and, what's more, I plan to remain this way for a very long time to come." He clasped his hands behind his bare bottom and began to pace at the head of the table. Several of his generals took cautious second glances from under the bills of their caps at their leader's root-white, plump nudity.

"You've got a good body," Doenitz added lamely.

There was another silence. Then Reichsführer of the Schutzstaffel Himmler swallowed hard. "You plan to go around like that . . . regularly?" he asked.

"Yes, I do. And what of it?"

"If I might make so bold as to point out—"

"Yes?"

"Well, if people saw you, it might . . . it might embarrass the Reich."

Hitler looked hard at Himmler for a moment. "I'm surprised at you, Herr Himmler," he said quietly. "I thought you were a man of greater vision. Do we actually care about the Reich?"

"No, Führer."

"Do we care whether the Reich lasts a thousand years or twenty minutes?"

"No, Führer."

"Do we care in the slightest about this red herring of a war which we have thrown across the path of the non-Aryan world?"

"No, Führer."

"What is our real goal, our secret dream that no one else knows? What is this dream that we have dreamed together so many times?"

"Our dream is that the Third Reich, in the person of its Führer, Adolf Hitler, shall become the greatest plot device the world has ever known," Himmler said, in the singsong tone of one repeating an oft-recited maxim.

"The greatest plot device the world has ever known!" Hitler suddenly shouted. "A mighty dream! For which we should strive mightily!"

He turned to Goebbels. "Tell me, Herr Minister," he asked, "how goes it with the Plot Restructurement Corps? Are you meeting with success?"

"Excellent success, Führer," Goebbels answered, keeping his eyes with some effort on his leader's face. "We have already removed the structurally impure elements from all the major literary works of the English and have inserted fear-of-Nazi-menace as the main instrument of plot. Might I read you a sample of our recent work?"

"Please."

An aide appeared at Goebbels' side with a manuscript, and Goebbels read:

THE ELSINORE AGENDA
By William Shakespeare

BERNARDO: Who's there?

FRANCISCO: Nay, answer me. Stand and unfold yourself.

BERNARDO: Long live the king!

FRANCISCO: Bernardo?

BERNARDO: He.

FRANCISCO: You come most carefully upon your hour.

BERNARDO: 'Tis now struck twelve. Get thee to bed, Francisco.

FRANCISCO: For this relief much thanks. 'Tis bitter cold, and I am sick at heart.

BERNARDO: Have you had quiet guard?

FRANCISCO: Not a mouse stirring.

BERNARDO: That's good. Because the Führer is a nut on the subject of Denmark, and we're supposed to watch out for Nazis.

FRANCISCO: Gee that's right. Thanks for reminding me. I sure hope we don't see any Nazis around here—

"Enough!" cried Hitler, stopping Goebbels with a gesture of his hand. "I can see that your corps has made most satisfactory progress, and you will persevere until every plot ever devised has fallen before you!"

For a moment, Hitler examined his waist, absentmindedly pinching its folds. "Now, gentlemen," he said, "we must look to the future. Consider Napoleon. He thought he would be an agent of plot for centuries. Yet today hardly anybody ever uses him, even once in a while just to give a story a nudge. And why is that? Because that military genius, that greatest general of modern times, that master of nations, did not possess the will to disrobe, even just down to his briefs. Alexander the Great, Caesar, Genghis Khan—did any one of them have the moral strength to walk about this world as naked as he came into it?"

"You're covered with goose bumps, Führer," Goering interrupted. "Can I get you a shawl or something?"

"What would you have me do?" Hitler asked, ignoring him. "Would you have me stare unseeing out a window, like some petty plot functionary? The American Presidents think that all they have to do is be President and stare out a window and someone will write about them. They sit in their Oval Offices and indulge their bad moods and think that is enough. But would any of them ever go nude? In the Oval Office? Right at the beginning of a story? Of course not. Because they are a mongrel race." He grabbed a book from one of the bookcases that lined the conference room from floor to ceiling. "Tell me—is this how you would have literature use your Führer?" He began to read:

THE TAFT ENIGMA
Chapter 1

President William Howard Taft, the twenty-seventh President of the United States, stared savagely out of the windows of the Oval Office. The fresh smell of flowers and other plants in the Rose Garden wafted to him through the same window that he was looking out of, and other windows as well, all of which were open in the pleasant weather, but the smell did not cheer the President up that much, because he was thinking about various things that concerned his Administration (1909–13) that were not going the way he wanted them to. Even if the weather was nice, it didn't make any difference to President Taft, because he was unhappy.

So what if the weather was great—President Taft still had things to worry about, because he was President. "Damn it," he thought, "here I have been a prominent Ohio jurist, United States Solicitor General, Dean of the Cincinnati Law School, author of the policy of 'dollar diplomacy' in China and Latin America, and still I cannot persuade Congress to pass my bill providing for the creation of the parcel-post system." President Taft began to pace back and forth like an animal of some kind in that office where so many Presidents had paced before him.

An aide wearing the type of clothes aides wore in Taft's day came in. "Should I close the window, Mr. President? Is that too much air on you?" he asked.

"What? Oh, I hadn't even noticed that the window was—"

"Forgive us, Führer! We were blind!" cried Himmler.

"We understand now, Führer!" cried Goebbels.

Then, as one, the generals and ministers leaped to their feet, eyes shining, fingers fumbling with their buttons.

A READING LIST
FOR YOUNG WRITERS

When aspiring young authors come to me and ask
what books I think it essential for a modern writer to
have read, I am hard pressed for an answer. I dislike
talking about writing, because I believe that the job of
a writer is to write rather than talk, and that real writing is something so deep within one that any discussion profanes it. In addition, I have a profound dis-
trust of lists—the ten-best this, the twenty-worst that.
Such lists strike me as a characteristically American
oversimplification of life's diversity. Like most writers
of any experience, I fear making lists simply because
I fear leaving something out. Young writers, however,
can be very insistent (I have found), and, as no less an
authority than Flaubert once said, "what a scholar one
might be if one knew well merely some half a dozen

books." So I have decided to tackle this difficult task despite my misgivings. The following six works are ones that I believe every writer—in fact, every educated person—should know as well as he knows his own name and telephone number:

Remembrance of Things Past. Marcel Proust's lyric, luminous evocation of lost time is arguably the greatest novel of the twentieth century. Moving from private to public scope, from the narrator's boyhood in the small provincial town of Combray, through the glittering salons of the Faubourg-Saint-Germain in Paris, to the sun-blinded hotels and beaches of Hawaii's Diamond Head, this monumental work has as its intent the precise description of Time itself. Time is as much a character in the book as the narrator, Marcel, or his ex-wife, Valerie. When Marcel meets Valerie on a flight to Honolulu, she is much changed since he saw her last; now she is an international diamond smuggler, and the mob has put a hundred-thousand-dollar price on her head. Again, Time is the genie who reveals to Marcel unguessed secrets about a woman with whom he was once deeply in love. Many writers have imitated Proust's generous, untrammeled, multihued prose; none has ever equaled it.

Madame Bovary. In Emma Bovary, Flaubert created a character who will live as long as there are books and readers. Flaubert, we are told, wrote slowly and carefully; I try to take the same care when I read him. In the marvelous scene when Emma first discovers that the petit-bourgeois pharmacist, Homais, is operating a baby-stealing ring, the intricate chiastic imagery switches from the look of horror on Emma's face to the happy, gurgling laughter of the innocent babies in their makeshift cribs in the garage behind the drug-store. Flaubert's genius for the accumulation of observed detail in delineating character showed the way for many later writers—particularly James Joyce.

War and Peace. Tolstoy's epic novel of Russia during the Napoleonic era is, in essence, a parable about the power of the media. Pierre Bezuhov is the ambitious young reporter who will go to any length to get a story —including murder. What he doesn't know is that Natasha Rostov, Moscow's feared "Dragon Lady," wants Pierre iced, and the hit man is Prince Andrei, Pierre's old college roommate! No writer who ever lived possessed a surer sense of plot than Tolstoy.

Buddenbrooks. Meet Antonie. She's beautiful. She's talented. She's sexy. She's the daughter of rich German businessman Jean Buddenbrook. And she's a walking time bomb. Somebody wants her dead, and she has been infected with a deadly virus that takes twenty-four hours to work. Half the city of Frankfurt goes underground looking for the antidote, and the police, in desperation, join forces with the mob. Author Thomas Mann interweaves these many strands so effortless / that it is easy to see why he, along with Proust and Joyce, was considered one of the three main architects of twentieth-century literature.

Bleak House. This is the one with the car chase, right? And the exploding helicopter at the end? Excellent! A neglected book but one of Dickens's best.

Ulysses. Stephen Dedalus, star of James Joyce's *Ulysses,* teams up with twelve beautiful lady truckers to find the madman responsible for a series of brutal murders. When Stephen himself becomes a suspect, he turns to his old buddy from 'Nam, Jim Rockford.

Jim comes up with a great plan, which is to pretend that Stephen is dead and to plant a fake obituary in his brother-in-law's newspaper. Then Jim, Angel, Molly Bloom, Buck Mulligan, Rocky, Stephen, and the twelve beautiful lady truckers fly over to Dublin, Stephen's hometown. It is St. Patrick's Day, and in the mass of people the killer escapes. Then the action moves to New Orleans, where Mardi Gras is in full swing. Then it's down to Rio, for Carnaval. All this time, Joyce keeps the reader informed as to what is going on inside each character's head.

My list is, of course, only a beginning. View it as the foundation of a literary mind; do not mistake it for the edifice itself. If you approach these books with passion, with an eye to their symmetries and harmonies and violent dissonances, you will not necessarily learn how to write. But you will certainly come nearer an understanding of what it is, gloriously, to read.

THE KILLION

At a little after noon on Friday, August 6, Marcie Chang, anchorwoman on TV 8's *Newsbeaters* evening news show, picked up her envelope at the pay window on the studio's fifth floor, bought a ham-salad sandwich and a cup of coffee from the lunch wagon in the hall, and took the elevator back to her office on the tenth floor. Sitting down at her desk, she tore open the envelope, which contained the first payment of the lucrative new contract that the station had offered her in the spring. She took one look at the check and collapsed. She was dead before her face hit the desk top. A few minutes later, TV reporter Kerri Corcoran, a colleague and friend, came into Marcie's office, saw her, looked at the check she still held in her hand, and crumpled, lifeless, to the floor. The same fate met the receptionist who came to Marcie's office to find out why she wasn't answering her phone, and the building security guard, who was summoned by the cleaning woman after she had noticed the pile of bodies.

Nor was that the end. In quick succession, three police officers, a fireman, a newspaper reporter, and a pathologist from Mount Sinai were added to the death list. Alarmed public-health officials called on the Institute for Catastrophe Control in Princeton. With grim predictability, two of the institute's top scientists soon showed the seriousness of the challenge when they, too, were felled. Within forty-eight hours, scientists from the institute who had taken over the case were fairly certain that the fatal agent was the check that Marcie had picked up that Wednesday afternoon. They examined it through heavily tinted safety glasses, in sections, with no one scientist viewing the entire check. Within another forty-eight hours, Dr. Leo Wiedenthal, director of the institute, knew what he had on his hands. In a statement released to the press, he said that there was no evidence of a super-toxin or highly contagious disease on the fatal pay-check. Rather, he said, "Marcie Chang and the eleven other victims almost certainly died as a result of what they *saw* on the check. Through a computer error, Marcie's check was made out to an extremely high number. Apparently, the computer made Marcie's check out to the sum of one killion dollars. The killion, as every mathematician knows, is a number so big that it kills you."

Since the days of Archimedes, man has known that numbers could attain great size. The Greeks could count up to a million, and the Romans, in their turn, made it to a billion and a trillion. Then man had to wait almost fifteen centuries, until the gilded arms of the Renaissance had flung open the shutters of the Dark Ages, before he could move on to a billion trillion, a million billion trillion, and, finally, a zillion. In 1702, Sir Isaac Newton, father of the theory of universal gravitation, experimented with numbers as high as a million billion trillion zillion, at one point even getting up to a bazillion. These experiments convinced him of the theoretical possibility of the existence of the killion. He stopped his experiments abruptly when, as the numbers approached one killion, he found himself becoming very sick. The German mathematician Karl Friedrich Gauss, hearing about Newton's discovery from someone he met at a party, was so upset by the thought of a killion that he made up his own numbers, called Gaussian numbers. These were numbers that could get big, but not that big. Unfortunately, Gauss's brave attempt to develop a risk-free numerical system wound up on the scrap heap of failed theories. In the early twentieth century, Albert Einstein made some calculations that brought him right to the very threshold of the killion. But here even Einstein halted. Probably the smartest scientist who ever lived, Einstein also had a great, abiding affection for life. After the invention of the computer, it was Einstein who insisted that each one be equipped with a governor that would shut it off automatically if it ever approached a killion. Were it not for Einstein's farsightedness, the dawn of the computer age might have had frightening consequences for mankind.

So what went wrong in the affair of Marcie Chang's deadly paycheck? Why did the network computer, run-

·ning a routine payroll program, make an error that no computer had ever made before? To understand this question, it is important to understand how a computer works. People unfamiliar with computers sometimes find it helpful to think of them as fairly good-sized, complicated things. Computers range in size from as small as a motel ice bucket to as large as an entertainment complex like New Jersey's Meadowlands, including the parking lot. Inside, a computer will have a short red wire hooked to a terminal at one end and to another terminal at the other end. Then there will be a blue wire also hooked to terminals at either end, and then a green wire, and then a yellow wire, then an orange wire, then a pink wire, and so on.

This particular computer was so big that when expert technicians began to disassemble it to find out what was the matter with it, they soon had more wires, terminals, and other parts lying around than they knew what to do with. The technicians spread the parts all over the floor of an unused equipment shed, and finally they found one that they identified as the governor—the little safety device that could trace its lineage back to Einstein's terrifying vision on that rainy February afternoon in Munich so many years ago. When they examined it closely, they discovered the problem. It was completely covered with gray stuff, kind of similar to the gray stuff that collects on rotary hot-dog grills. There was so much gray stuff that the little armature that was supposed to fit into a V-shaped groove on this other armature couldn't fit in at all. No one knew where the gray stuff could have come from, so there was nowhere to fix the blame. That did not change the fact that a small amount of gray stuff you could blow from your palm with one light breath had cost twelve human lives.

In the aftermath of the tragedy, many people asked, "How can such tragedies be prevented in the future?" Well, you could give your paycheck to the bank teller every week without looking at it—taking such risks is what bank tellers are paid for. But then you would never know how much money you had. You could move to a country where people have never heard of computers. But that might be awfully far away, and it might be years before you felt comfortable there. You could vacuum computers at least three times a week to remove any foreign matter. But, on the other hand, what if that didn't work?

One hard, indisputable truth remains: There is nothing anybody can do about the killion. It is not a person, or a product, or an institution, and so need answer to no one. It will always be out there, in the far range of mathematics, where space bends and parallel lines converge, and I don't know what all. In the end, the best you can really do is hope that if the killion gets anyone, the person it gets won't be you.

JUST A COUNTRY BOY

If you think that when you look at me you're looking at rock, rhythm and blues, jazz, classical, or pop, then you are wrong, because I am country from my head down to my boots. If you're looking at me, then by definition you are looking at country. When I was in my early teens, the great Hank Williams told me, "Son, you ain't country unless you've looked at a lot of miles over the back end of a mule." Unfortunately, because of conflicts in my schedule at the time, I did not have a chance to look at as many miles over the back end of a mule as I would have liked to. Hank, however, made some excellent videotapes of miles with the back end of a mule in the foreground, and I spent countless hours screening those tapes.

Excuse me. That's my phone.

Sorry. That was the lonesome highway calling me. It calls me just about every day at this time. Just about every day, I get calls from the lonesome highway, the gentle Southern summer breezes, my Smoky Mountain memories, and that lonesome freight-train whistle's whine. If I'm not in, they leave messages. I don't mind all these calls, because they remind me that I'm just a country boy and that's all I'll ever be. (Although sometimes that lonesome freight-train whistle's whine can be a little irritating. I pick up the phone and all I hear is this whine.)

I like it when the lonesome highway calls, because for a long time it has been my only friend. I don't know exactly why I always keep moving on down the road. One reason might be that I've got a different girl in every town you can name. There's a Cajun Queen down in Baton Rouge who usually tries to avoid me. And in North Dallas there's a rich man's daughter who says she doesn't like me that much. In old San Antone there's a dark-eyed señorita who didn't have a very good time with me, while up in Memphis there are several Tennessee belles whose feelings toward me are lukewarm at best. I tell them all the same thing: "I am not the kind of man to hang around with any one woman for too long, because I am always chasing rainbows. So please bear that in mind." That is not an easy thing to tell someone (particularly if you have to yell it through her locked door), but I know myself well enough to say that it is nothing more or less than the simple truth.

I am country today, and I was country this time last year—I have photographs to prove it. I was country back before Hollywood brought Texas to New York and imitation drugstore cowboys turned up all over the Sunset Strip. I was country in '80, '79, '78, '77, '76 —it doesn't matter how far back you want to go. I was country when country wasn't cool. In fact, I was country back when it was forbidden by law in most states and the federal government turned a blind eye to this blatant violation of the rights of its people. I was country back when if you were intelligent enough to buy beer and you tried to be country you could be fined, or even imprisoned. Now it is hard to believe that such times ever existed.

My daddy was just a simple backwoods art director (B.F.A., Rhode Island School of Design) out of Checotah, Oklahoma. He raised me right. He insisted that I spend at least three hours out of every day honkytonking, and he was very strict. I had to bring him bar tabs from as many places as I could, to prove I had really bar-hopped. He also made me practice cheating and slipping around behind my wife's back. Of course, I was much too young to be married, so we pretended I was married to Yeller, my dog. Then I would go over to our neighbors' yard and sweet-talk their dog, Blue. "What part of heaven did you fall from, angel?" I'd say. "No, no, no!" Daddy would holler. "Say it like you mean it! Put some ol' country sorghum in your voice!" And he'd make me try it again and again, until I finally had Yeller howling with jealousy. At the time, I have to admit, I hated my daddy for being so hard on me, but now I understand what he was doing, and I thank him for it.

Many of the experiences of my life were like that; I did not understand at the time that they were molding me into pure country, which is what I am today. Like when I went to tennis camp with Bob Wills and several of the Texas Playboys. Or the time I made a snow sculpture with Ernest Tubb. Or the time I went on a two-month tour of the canals of Europe with Jimmie Rodgers, the Singing Brakeman. Each of these experiences taught me a little bit more about what country really means.

So when people who don't have the benefit of similar experiences ask me "What is country?" I don't know what to tell them. Country is so many things. It's knowing how to find the country station on your radio dial. It's watching the TV pages to see when the next country-music awards show is on. It's knowing the location of the aisle labeled "Country" at your record store . . . It's all these things, and yet, somehow, it's more. It's ineffable, really. And when my friends, all of them country "kickers" like myself, and I watch people who just plain *ain't* country trying to pretend they are —when we watch them fumble with their radios searching for a country station—well, then we just smile. Because if you're not country, then there's nothing you can do about it. Because real, down-home country is something that comes from the heart. Because there is no way if you aren't country that you can ever possibly become country—certainly not without working at it for, at the very least, seven to ten years.

FROM THERE TO HERE

As a child of the sixties, I never tire of attending reunions of my friends and comrades who struggled together through that exciting era. My affinity group at the march on the Pentagon, at the Chicago Convention, and at the Boston Common still gets together once a month to reminisce. The guys in my men's rap group, veterans of so many coffee-and-cigarette late-night sessions in those distant Summers of Love, meet four times a year at a restaurant in Chinatown. And as for the "heads" who went looking for America on the Merry Pranksters' bus—Kesey, myself, Mountain Girl, Hassler, Zonker, Speed Limit, and the rest—we convene the first Tuesday of every month, no matter the weather, at twelve noon in the lobby of the Airway Motor Inn, beside LaGuardia Airport. At all these reunions, we sixties survivors talk, compare notes, and wonder at the odd arcs our lives have described since the days when we awoke every morning expecting to find a world transformed by love, radiant and utopian, waiting on our doorstep.

For the most part, we find that the years have softened us. Now we can see the gray areas, whereas, before, all we could see was black and white. We are not so much saddened by these changes as we are gently bemused. No, things didn't turn out the way we thought they would. But then neither did we. We grew, nudged by forces both inside and outside ourselves, forces that we did not take into account at the time. Personal fulfillment in such areas as love, sexuality, careers, and coping gradually overrode the slogans of the sixties. The next thing we knew, we weren't the kids anymore—we were the adults, with kids of our own.

These days, when we get together to marvel at the major and minor miracles that brought us from there to here, we find that our conversation always seems to return to the children. Rather than bemoaning the shattered dreams of our revolutionary youth, more and more we find ourselves amazed at the unanticipated miracle of this new generation. Sixty million Americans born since the Beatles released "Rubber Soul"! Sixty million for whom the Berkeley Free Speech Movement is a historical event as remote as the Korean War! These kids are so different from us, and yet they're so wonderful, too. They're committed, competent, hardworking, goal-oriented—all the things we weren't. So levelheaded, so matter-of-fact, so accepting of the way the world is, so undismayed.

Not for them the wild caroming from rock music to drugs to gurus to radical politics which characterized the generation of the sixties; today's kids know what they want, and they know how they're going to get it. With all they have seen, they have a wisdom that many of their parents are still seeking.

I know my friends sometimes may think I'm a bit of a pain when we're trading snapshots, the way I go on about my nephews Zachariah and Noah. They're my sister's kids from her first and second marriages, and I can't help bragging about them. Those kids really keep me sane. Surprisingly, I find very often it is *I* who learn from *them.* They have a terrific ability to deflate their elders' pretensions and follies with a sense of humor that is refreshingly down to earth. For example, when we ride the subway I always retreat into my shell, stare at my feet, and put on a blank expression, like so many other numbed adults. Not my nephews. They'll stroll up and down the car, looking into the shopping bag of one passenger, mussing the hair of another. They'll remove the glasses from this one and then replace them upside down, or they'll pull up the shirt collar of that one and read the label. If they see an attractive woman, why, they'll give her a pinch or a pat. They're so in touch with their feelings—their anger, particularly. If someone laughs at them, they'll give him a lick over the head with a golf club that they carry just for that purpose, and then take his box radio. How they come up with these things I can't imagine. They have such marvelous savvy. They know where to sell gold chains, what arcades in Times Square are best for meeting older men from New Jersey, what day of the month the Social Security checks arrive. Being around them is a twenty-four-hour-a-day experience in wonder. I can never tell what they're going to do next. I've long ago stopped trying to figure them out. All I do is love them, watch them, listen to them, and try to let them teach me.

And what about us grownups—lapsed flower children, ex-peaceniks? Do we have anything to teach the kids of today? Can we tell them how it felt to live for an idea, to stand with arms linked against oppression and racism, to sing with our brothers and sisters about the world we were going to build? Sadly, we cannot— any more than our parents could tell us about their youth. And that is the irony: that the children of the eighties should help us to understand not only our own time but also our parents' (the children of the eighties' grandparents') time; because we, the parents of today, understand better why our parents acted toward us as they did when we look at our own children and see that in twenty years, when they have children of their own, they will understand us better —the way we now understand our parents better. And maybe then the kids of today will begin to understand the spirit of the sixties.

IGOR STRAVINSKY:
THE SELECTED PHONE CALLS

	NO	DATE	TIME	PLACE	AREA-NUMBER	RATE APPLIED	MIN	AMOUNT
(A)	1	MAR 5	1101PM	TO NEW ORLEANS LA	504 555-6872	DIALED NIGHT	38	6.45
(B)	14	JUN 7	1037AM	TO CUSTER SD	605 555-9722	DIALED DAY	25	10.69
(C)	7	SEP 27	739PM	TO NEW YORK NY	212 555-0362	DIALED EVENING	104	31.24
(D)	15	FEB 8	833PM	FROM BOSTON MA	COL 555-1992	OPER EVENING	29	10.22
	5	JAN 7	330PM	TO SAN FRAN CA	415 555-7710	DIALED DAY	1	.29
(E)	6	JAN 7	344PM	TO SAN FRAN CA	415 555-7710	" "	1	.29
	7	JAN 7	403PM	TO SAN FRAN CA	415 555-7710	" "	1	.29
	8	JAN 7	418PM	TO SAN FRAN CA	415 555-7710	" "	1	.29

Composer, conductor, critic, teacher, iconoclast, and grand old man, Igor Stravinsky bestrode this century like a colossus, with feet on two different continents. Already respected and popular in Europe for writing pieces like *Le Sacre du Printemps,* he became equally if not more famous in his adopted country of America. The many friends he made here remember him as a man of breathtaking talent, whether he was composing an epochal symphony or playing shadow puppets in the candlelight after a small dinner party. Like many other geniuses, he was generous, almost profligate, with his gifts. He would write beautiful phrases of music on restaurant napkins and give them to friends, acquaintances, even passersby. Thoughts bubbled forth from him in such a torrent that often when he

79

was sitting in his den writing a letter to a friend he would impulsively grab for the telephone, look up his friend's number in his address book while holding the phone to his ear with his shoulder, and dial. In a matter of seconds, he would be pouring out ideas that might have required days, even weeks, to travel through the mails. At the other end of the line, the friend would listen with delight as the great man went on, humming or singing at times, until finally he was "all talked out." Then Stravinsky would bid his grateful hearer goodbye, and, in the pleasant afterglow of inspiration, he would crumple up the unfinished letter, throw it in the wastebasket, and mix himself a cocktail.

Fortunately for us, his heirs, Stravinsky was a man aware of his place in history. With careful consideration for the students and biographers he knew would follow, he saved his telephone bills from year to year, and before his death he donated the entire corpus to the K-Tel Museum of the Best Composers Ever. What a fascinating picture these phone bills paint! With their itemized lists of long-distance calls and charges, they are like paper airplanes thrown to us from the past, providing a detailed record of the seasons of Stravinsky's mind in the multihued pageant of life as he lived it on a daily basis. And what better time for a close examination of the treasures his phone bills contain than this, the year after the centennial of Stravinsky's birth? (Actually, the centennial year itself would probably have been better, but even though this year might not be as good a time as last year, still, it is almost as good.) Now let us turn to the documents:

Ⓐ This call, made not long after Stravinsky moved to America and had his phone hooked up, shows him adjusting quickly to the ways of his new country. With scenes of Old World poverty fresh in his memory, he has prudently waited to place the call until 11:01 p.m., the very moment when the lowest off-peak rates go into effect. Such patience and calculation indicate a call that was professional rather than social in nature. Almost certainly, the recipient was Stravinsky's fellow composer Arnold Schoenberg. It was common knowledge that Schoenberg often vacationed in New Orleans, where he enjoyed the food, the atmosphere, and the people. Stravinsky may have found out from a mutual friend where Schoenberg was staying and then surprised him with this call. Always one to speak his mind, Stravinsky probably began by telling Schoenberg that his dodecaphonic methods of musical composition were a lot of hooey. Very likely, Schoenberg would have bristled at this, and may well have reminded Stravinsky that great art, like the Master's own *Sacre,* need not be immediately accessible. Stravinsky then probably made a smart remark comparing Schoenberg's methods to the methods of a troop of monkeys with a xylophone and some hammers. This probably made Schoenberg pretty mad, and it is a testament to the great (albeit hidden) regard each man had for the other that the call lasted as long as it did. Possibly, Schoenberg just held his temper and said something flip to defuse the situation, and then Stravinsky moved on to another subject. Inasmuch as they never spoke again, this intense thirty-eight-minute phone conversation may represent a seminal point in the history of twentieth-century music theory.

Ⓑ This call is of particular interest to the student because of its oddity. One is compelled to ask, "Who did Stravinsky know in Custer, South Dakota?" He never went there; none of his friends or relatives ever went there; the town has no symphony orchestra. So why did he call there? It is hard to believe that on a June morning the sudden urge for a twenty-five-minute chat with a person in Custer, South Dakota, dropped onto Stravinsky out of the blue. No, we must look elsewhere for an explanation. Two possibilities suggest themselves: (1) an acquaintance of the composer, perhaps an occasional racquetball partner, a fan, even a delivery boy from the supermarket, comes by the Stravinskys', sees no one is in, and takes the opportunity to make a long-distance call and stick someone else with the tab; or (2) the telephone company made an error. In either event, Stravinsky should not have paid the ten dollars and sixty-nine cents, and I believe it was taken from him unfairly, just as much as if a mugger had stolen it from him on the street.

Ⓒ Here we have a side of the composer's personality which we must face unflinchingly if we are to be honest. Every man has a dark side; this is his. On an evening in late September, just after dinner, Stravinsky placed a call to New York and talked for a hundred and four minutes. *A hundred and four minutes!* That's almost two hours! As one ear got tired and he switched the phone to the other, he obviously did not realize how inconsiderate he was being. It was as if he were the only person in the whole world who needed to use the phone. What if his wife wanted to make a call? What if somebody was trying to call him from a pay phone, dialing every five minutes, only to hear the busy signal's maddening refrain? Surely, after an hour or so he could have found a polite way to hang up. Surely, he could have at least made an effort to think of someone other than himself. But he didn't—he just kept yakking along, without a worry or a care, for over one hundred selfish minutes.

We should always remember that the perfection we demand of our heroes they cannot, in reality, ever attain.

Ⓓ Calling Stravinsky collect would seem to be the act of either a madman or a genius—or both. Yet here before us is the evidence that not only did someone pull such a stunt but Stravinsky actually went along with it and accepted the charges. In all likelihood, the caller was a young admirer, possibly a music student (Boston is known for its many music schools), who found himself in the middle of a creative crisis with nowhere else to turn. It shows how nice Stravinsky could be when he wanted to be that he gave the young man a shoulder to cry on, as well as some helpful encouragement. The disconsolate youth probably said that he despaired of ever finding an entry-level position as a composer, and that even if he did he was sure he would never make very much per week. Stravinsky may have gently reminded the lad that music is not a job but a vocation—which its true disciples cannot deny—and he may have added that a really good composer can earn a weekly salary of from eight hundred to one thousand dollars. Comforted, the student probably hung up and returned to his work with renewed dedication, and later went on to become Philip Glass or Hugo Winterhalter or André Previn. As success followed success, the young student (now adult) would always remember the time a great man cared enough to listen.

Ⓔ This delightful series of calls reveals the Master at his most puckish. The time is a drab afternoon in midwinter; Stravinsky is knocking around the house at loose ends, possibly with a case of the post-holiday blahs. Maybe he starts idly leafing through a San Francisco telephone directory. Then, perhaps, a sudden grin crosses his face. He picks a number at random and dials. One ring. Two rings. A woman's voice answers. Stravinsky assumes a high, squeaky voice. "Is Igor there?" he asks. Informed that he has the wrong number, he hangs up.

Fourteen minutes pass. Then he calls back. In a low voice this time, he repeats his question: "Hi. Is Igor there?" Sounding a bit surprised, the woman again replies in the negative.

Nineteen minutes later, again Stravinsky dials the San Francisco number. Now his voice takes on a rich Southern accent: "Hello, ma'am, is Igor there?"

"No, there's nobody by that name here," the woman says, by this time truly perplexed.

Stravinsky lets fifteen minutes go by. Then he is ready to deliver the classic punch line, which he has orchestrated as carefully as the crescendo in one of his most beautiful symphonies. He redials the number. The woman answers, a trace of annoyance coloring her tone. The great composer waits one beat; then, in his normal voice, he says, "Hello, this is Igor. Have there been any calls for me?"

An artist such as this comes along only once in a great while. Had he done nothing else but accumulate his remarkable portfolio of phone bills, he would merit our consideration. But, of course, he did much more than that, in music as well as in other areas. We who are his contemporaries cannot presume to judge him in his totality; that task we must leave for future ages blessed with a vision far greater than today's.

TO THE HEAVENS,
AND BEYOND

World literature is like a great river, with its source situated somewhere in the dim past not far from man's own beginnings and its terminus ever receding before us in the mists that veil the destiny of our race. Some men, such as Dickens or Tolstoy, ride the middle of the river, and, in turn, contribute their own works to the surging of its flow. Other writers, whose names and works you have never heard of, might be compared to small drops of water on the waves along the river's edge. But of those many thousand souls who share the mysterious urge to set words on paper it might be said that, be they famous or be they unknown, all are part of this same river. To a greater or lesser degree, they all partake of its waters in the high communion of their art. Why is it, then, that in the broad spectrum of humanity writers should be the meanest, the pettiest, the most jealous, mudslinging, backstabbing, self-centered, conceited people who ever lived? It is only within the last few months that I have come to an understanding of just how bad writers can be. The event that really opened my eyes was when the National Aeronautics and Space Administration (NASA) selected me, out of a multitude of other writers, to participate in their five-year Community in Space program on an orbiting station twenty thousand miles above the earth. I won't bother to review all the nasty, sniping attacks on me which many of the unsuccessful candidates for the position have given vent to in national publications. I only wonder if the space colonists (all of them leaders in their fields) who were chosen to represent the other professions had to endure such a torrent of abuse from their colleagues. My feeling is that they did not.

It has been written that my selection was the result of backstairs political maneuvers on my part. When you see that written anywhere, you will know for sure that the author has never met me, and that, in fact, he knows less about me than he does about the President of Togo. As anyone with even a slight acquaintance with me will tell you, I am a man who was born, and has remained, a truthteller; that is the very core of my nature. To speak anything other than the truth is an act of which I am almost physically incapable. So, as it happens, the hypocrisy, flattery, and glad-handing that grease the social wheels for millions of my fellows are skills far beyond my ken. The unblinking light of my regard falls the same upon everyone (including myself) without fear or favor. This troublesome honesty of mine has stood in the way of my advancement more times than I can count, but I accept its disadvantages without complaint; you see, it's just the way I am.

Now, to set the record straight, and to put a stop to the half-truths and rumors, I will tell how NASA came to choose me. I am afraid it is a simple story, entirely devoid of exciting secret schemes. One day, I picked up a newspaper and saw the announcement that NASA was looking for top members of some forty different professions to live for five years in a creative community housed in an orbiting space station. By chance, I was unemployed at the time, and eager for new challenges. I rushed down to the Pentagon, found the offices of the Air Force, and put my name on the sign-up sheet. My name was not at the top of the list; nor was it at the bottom. Then I was told that anyone who wished to apply had sixty days to submit the necessary recommendations, as well as a sample of his or her most recent work. I gave much thought to the sample I would submit. I wanted it to have a little something for everyone; I wanted it to be fresh; I wanted it to grapple with large themes. So, first of all, I went out and bought a middle-sized motor home with my own savings. I was convinced that I must leave behind the comfortable routines of my life up to that point. After much painful soul-searching, I decided to split once and for all from my estranged wife. I had lost her boyfriend's phone number, so I left a note on her car informing her of my intention. Then, just to be on the safe side, I also broke up with the guy at the newsstand, the boy who serviced my vehicle, and a tolltaker on the New Jersey Turnpike. I set off down the highway with her recriminations still ringing in my ears.

My first stop was New England. I picked a comfortable campsite and got right to work. Immediately I was pleased to notice that the stately, brooding shadows of Hawthorne, Thoreau, and Emerson fell across my typewriter as I chronicled life in the land of the three-martini lunch, where Ivy League–educated denizens of sprawling bedroom communities improvise unconventional marriages in the sexual confusion of the later twentieth century. That was fun; but I began to worry that I was speaking in a voice that could do with a bit more American authenticity. So I headed out on Interstate 90. As I passed Buffalo, I could feel my voice becoming more authentic. Cleveland—even more authentic. Then Chicago. Aah—authenticity was now all around me. I spent eleven days on the outskirts of that city, creating, growing, and learning. (For example, did you know that Chicago is actually *not* the windiest city in this country? In fact, it's rather far down the list.) Then I was back on the highway. When I reached the Far West, I noticed that my prose suddenly became as vast and brawling as the landscape that surrounded it. Eventually, through a careful budgeting of time and money, I was able to pursue my stylistic development in forty-six of the fifty states. Then I drove back to Washington, to type up my final copy and turn it in. Reading it over, I discovered that I'd found a large theme, all right. That theme was America itself.

The news that I had made the final cut absolutely floored me. I was even more stunned when I showed up at the Air Force offices and got a look at the nine other finalists. Among them were some of the most famous writers in the country, people whose names you would recognize in an instant. We were all given a mandatory essay question to complete in three hours. I was sure I'd be over my head in competition the likes of this, but I resolved to do my best. Our springboard topic was "The World's Greatest Dad." I chewed the eraser on my pencil for a moment, and then my hand began fairly flying across the pages of my blue book.

I shall always remember the day I found out that I'd been selected, because it was one of the happiest days of my life—and one of the saddest. The telegram found me at my campsite outside Bethesda. I screamed for joy; I jumped from my motor home; I took Mrs. Main, the campsite manager, in my arms and waltzed her around her office. But she had to get on with her work, so I called one of my closest friends, a novelist and essayist, to ask him to have a few beers with me in celebration. When I told him my news, a chill came into his voice. I knew for the first time that loneliness which must always walk hand in hand with the successful.

Soon, however, my gloom was dispersed in the whirlwind of events preceding our takeoff, which was only a month away. First, there was a picnic to meet the other future space colonists, at the beautiful home of an Air Force colonel in McLean, Virginia. I met many people of amazing intellect whose contributions to mankind had won them fame the world over, and I also met many whose fame was limited to only a small circle. Without exception, every single one was just as nice and friendly as anybody you'd ever want to talk to. We compared values and life styles in very stimulating exchanges as we helped ourselves to the sumptuous barbecue. At one point, I was standing around playing Jarts with a Nobel Prize-winning physicist, a Nobel Prize-winning chemist, and a famous international photojournalist. I turned to the chemist and said, "Pinch me, will you? I can't believe this is real!"

The next weeks passed in a frantic rush of orientation sessions, group discussions, weightlessness training (the space station has artificial gravity, but this was just in case), packing, final details, and goodbyes to loved ones. At last came the morning when we were standing with our suitcases on the concrete apron next to the space-shuttle launch pad at Cape Canaveral. There were too many of us to go all at once, so the shuttle had to make two trips. The bunch I went with had a ball. It was really something to watch the older fellows, whose gray hairs bespoke their eminence, as they anticipated liftoff with eyes dancing like those of a young boy on his first roller-coaster ride. The flight was the thrill of a lifetime for everybody. We arrived at the space station with spirits as high as our actual altitude in miles, if not higher.

I know that some of my literary colleagues back on the ground enviously imagine that we're luxuriating in plush surroundings up here, with nothing to do but work and enjoy. Well, I hate to shatter their illusions, but our quarters on the space station are no more ritzy than your average family motel room. Our needs are well provided for, but we don't live like millionaires, either. The room assigned to me is actually one of the smaller ones. (NASA gave everybody rooms on the basis of a system that I'm sure was fair, even though some people have rooms twice the size of mine.) I have a small radio, but no television. I don't mind that, because television, with its tendency to turn all human emotions into cup custard, is an aspect of modern culture which I abhor. Besides, we have our own fifty-seat movie theater—the only feature of our space station which I guess you might call luxurious. Sometimes we get to see first-run movies, and that suits me just fine, because I am a movie nut. Of course, life here is not without its annoying little technical problems, or "glitches," as we call them. The day we arrived, one of the station's outside thrust-reversers was screwed up, and everything kept tilting back and forth. I was in the midst of unpacking, putting pencils in my pencil holder, when suddenly things started to tilt, and the pencil holder toppled and all my pencils went scattering on the floor. Then, for some strange reason the water they brought up to use for drinking and showering turned out to be hard water; that is, water with high mineral content. I don't know why they didn't get regular water—some bureaucratic snafu, most likely. The water tasted O.K., but when you shampooed with it, no matter how hot you turned it up, it would not rinse your hair completely. After a few weeks of this kind of shampooing, all of us were walking around with hair that hung in lifeless strands. We were a pretty droopy-looking group, and morale began to suffer. Then NASA took the problem in hand and announced that they were adding another member to the Space Community. The new member was a serviceman from one of the leading water-softener companies. (I don't have to tell you which one—they have already blown their own horn loud enough, with their "Water Softener to America's Space Program" ad campaign.) The shuttle made a special trip to bring this guy up, and, after some initial awkwardness, he fit in fine.

Writers on earth may envy me, but I wonder if they know how I envy them. How I would love a little of their privacy, their anonymity, their freedom to foster their creations away from the bright lights of national and world attention! Whenever the space station passes over Houston, there's a knock on my door. "Jerry—it's Mission Control on the phone. They want to talk to you." I know that this is just part of the routine. I know that the Houston boys have a flight schedule with a list of all our names with little boxes alongside, and all they want to do is put a little check in the box by my name indicating that they've talked to me, that I sound fine, etc. They ask me how the book is going, and I give them vague answers, and that satisfies them. They always mention the "great view." They've got the idea that a person looking at the "great view" from up here would naturally be inspired to write as nobody in history has ever written before. "Oh, what a view!" I always answer.

Let me tell you a few facts about this supposed "great view." In the first place, there is one window in this space station. One window for the entire space station. And it's not even that big a window—it's about the size of a picture window in an ordinary house. In the second place, most of the time the space station is rotated around in a direction where all you can see out the window is blackness and a couple of stars. Maybe if you stood there and waited for a few hours, you might see a meteor. And then during those times when the space station is rotated around toward earth, the window is always packed with people, and all you can see is the back of everybody's head.

Now, say I burst from my room one afternoon, my brain teeming with half-formed plots and characterizations, and I decide to take a short stroll. What I'm hoping for is the catalyst, the spark that will set the whole structure aglow from within. I walk to the window; earth is visible, if only I could see it through the crowd. The conversation goes like this:

"See that bump there? That's Long Island."

"Long Island isn't a bump. It's more like a line."

"O.K., then what is that bump?"

"Which one, the first bump or the second bump?"

"Not the first bump. I'm talking about the smaller bump. The first bump is New Brunswick."

My question is: Was it in measures such as these that the Muses sang to Virgil and, later, Dante? I, for one, doubt it very much.

The guys at Mission Control are put off easily enough, but once a month the President calls, and that's a whole different situation. It's quite a bit harder to kid him along. He knows all our names and he even recognizes our voices, and while he's talking I'm sure he's got a file on each one of us sitting on his desk in front of him. I never know for sure what he's going to say. He's a man who digs deeper; he didn't get to be President by accepting pat answers. The last couple of times we've talked, he's been getting curious about my work, and I really don't want to go into it. I could say to him, "Look, writing is a process that takes place far back in the dim recesses of the mind, where words emerge and then go away again in a manner that even the most skillful of authors cannot easily explain in person, let alone over long-distance radiophone." But I don't tell him that—I try to cooperate. Our last conversation, however, was a nightmare.

"Hi, Jerry, how's the writing going?" he says.

"Pretty good," I say.

"How many chapters so far?"

"Almost ten."

"Wow! That's great! That's really a lot! How many pages would that be?"

"Oh, about a hundred and fifty," I say.

"A hundred and fifty! Wow!"

"Well, I triple-space."

"Still . . ." he says. Then he says, "Tell me, Jerry, do you mind my asking? I was wondering about the angle you're taking on your material."

"Well . . . it's, uh . . . you might say it's kind of darkly comic," I stammer.

There is a long pause, while my muscles begin to knot up and my forehead grows as clammy as the bottom of a vegetable compartment in a refrigerator. "Well, I'm sure you're doing a terrific job, and I just want you to know how proud I and all other Americans are of you, and I know that you'll show the world that our country has writers who are second to none!" he says.

I rushed back to my room and threw myself face down on my bed. *Darkly comic!* That's not the half of it! That doesn't begin to describe it! The truth is that from page 1 right up to the very last page I've written so far my book is deeply, profoundly disturbing! Or, to be more exact, Chapter 1 is profoundly disturbing; Chapter 2 is both profoundly disturbing and upsetting; Chapter 3 is disturbing, upsetting, and alarming; in Chapter 4, I let up a little, and that one is merely disconcerting; Chapter 5 provides another short breather, and it is just troubling; but Chapter 6 goes right back to profoundly disturbing again, and I continue like that without any break at all from then on. When the President finds out what a sweeping indictment of our civilization I'm writing up here (and on the government's nickel, no less), he's likely to go through the roof. I wouldn't want to be around the Oval Office to watch, I can tell you that.

YOUR NUTRITION & YOU

This week's column is by way of apology to the many readers (too many, I'm afraid) whose unanswered letters sit in heaps in my study. Seems like ever since I published *If You Don't Like It, Don't Eat It* I've been fighting a losing battle to keep up my correspondence with thousands of people around the country who appreciate my plain-speaking approach to diet and health and who want to discuss their individual dietary plans with me. I wish I could answer every letter personally. I know all too well what it's like to wander alone in a wilderness of nutritional dogma. To those of you who find yourselves hopelessly confused by all the television diet gurus and esoteric health-food treatises, I say, Don't give up! Keep searching for the

97

eating program that's right for you—keep experimenting on yourselves and your families—and don't be afraid to buck the experts and their conventional wisdom! The following is only a small sampling from my mailbag, but I hope all my readers will see a little bit of themselves in the questions, and learn from my answers.

Q: For the past ten years, my husband and I have been lactovegetarians, and we believe it is the diet God intended man to follow. It gives us great vitality and alertness, as well as a feeling of inner calm. I can honestly say that I no longer feel even the slightest desire to eat meat of any kind—in fact, the thought actually makes me a bit ill. Nowadays, the only time I ever stray from my diet is when I get the urge for some polyvinyl chloride. I don't know why it is, but those little plasticized fibers have a flavor that I absolutely adore. Once a week or so, I'll go out to the waste disposal bins at the local electronics plant and come home with laundry bags full. Then I'll sprinkle the fibers on salads, main dishes, even desserts. When my husband teases me about this, I tell him that everybody is entitled to one delightfully sinful treat. Don't you agree?

A: Often many of us forget that our appetites are a natural extension of the needs of our biochemistries. When we feel a strong craving for one substance or another, it usually means that our bodies lack that substance, and we should replenish our supplies. In your case, your body is telling you that you have electronic circuitry with dangerously exposed wiring

98

somewhere inside you, and it's time to coat those wires with a reliable industrial insulator—like polyvinyl chloride fibers. Had you let yourself be ruled by your conscience, and denied yourself this "sinful treat," chances are you would now be suffering from debilitating electrical shorts. So go ahead, eat up, and *bon appétit!*

Q: As the mother of a large family, I see to it that we get three well-balanced meals each day, with plenty of meats and fish, fresh vegetables from our garden, and big, heaping bowlfuls of pure powdered Kepone (that stuff farmers used to spray on their crops sometimes from airplanes). Now if we could only get rid of this doggone twitching of the neck muscles which causes our heads to jerk violently at unpredictable intervals, everything would be perfect. Any suggestions?

A: Like all responsible members of the medical profession, I am often forced to admit that we do not yet have all the answers. I would need more details about your diet and overall health picture before I could make any definite statements about the symptom you describe. Could it be that you are getting too much vitamin D? If you are taking a D supplement and eating foods (such as dairy products) which have D added, that may be causing a buildup. Vitamin D is fat soluble and thus remains in the system, and it can be toxic in large amounts. Also, you may have a case of what we call "innocent" or "whimsical" twitching—a muscle contraction that the body performs every so often, apparently just for the fun of it. If your symptoms persist, you might try the following:

99

1. Lift with your legs, not your back, in order to distribute the strain more evenly.

2. Don't hesitate to ask for help with precision tasks such as passing a truck on the freeway or trimming the kids' hair.

3. Wear loose-fitting clothing.

These guidelines may not cure the condition, but they will at least make it easier to bear.

Q: Last year I decided to quit drinking, and I began to sample various nonalcoholic beverages looking for one I liked. Tomato juice with Tabasco, herb tea, carbon tetrachloride, soft drinks, Perrier and lime, reactor coolant, tonic water, hexachlorocyclopentadiene (C-56) on shaved ice, lemonade—I tried them all, but none seemed quite right. Then one evening I was at the home of a dry cleaner friend of mine and he offered me some chlorobenzene. Wow! I'd never tasted anything like it! It had a delicious, almondy flavor combined with a bracing, almost overpowering astringency that could make a man forget blended malt whiskies forever. Right then and there, it became my beverage of choice.

Since I've been on the wagon, I feel much better (aside from a pesky red rash on the backs of my legs, along with weight loss, dizziness, and this darn second row of teeth I've started to grow), but if it weren't for chlorobenzene, I'd probably have gone back to the bottle long ago. I'm wondering—why isn't this wonderful product on the shelves at my supermarket or beverage store? I am forced to purchase it from dry-cleaning supply houses.

•

A: Don't ask me—ask the high panjandrums at the Food and Drug Administration! They're the ones who have chlorobenzene trussed up in red tape that limits it to commercial use only. Notoriously finicky eaters themselves, these career bureaucrats delight in dictating the menu for all America. And of course, it is you and I, the consumer, who must suffer. We can only hope that one day our government will come to its senses and stop treating its citizens as if they were all still in short pants, incapable of making the simplest decision about their lives. As for that second row of teeth you've developed—remember that twice as many teeth means you should be brushing twice as long. Recent studies have shown a clear link between oral health and the health of the body as a whole.

Q: I love lead—have ever since I was a youngster. I was raised on crunchy lead-based paint flakes, bite-sized toy soldiers made of lead, and good old-fashioned lead pencils. Today my kids and grandkids live in a completely different world. When they want something to chew on, they reach for the modern acrylic-based paint flakes, or plastic army men, or ersatz fruit-flavored marking pens. I tell them they don't know what they're missing. They call me an old dinosaur. Then they say that they've heard lead is bad for you. This gravels me, because I've been eating lead for years and am in perfect shape, except for some minor central nervous system damage which causes me to walk in tight circles. I'm all the time trying to get them to try a little lead, and they're always trying to get me to cut down. Neither of us will budge an inch. Who's right, them or me?

•

A: If lead is harmful to human beings, this is the first I've heard of it. I suppose if you ate enough of it, it might be, but you'd have to eat a tremendous amount, much more than any one person is likely to want. You might ask your young relatives: If lead is so harmful, why did the Romans, rulers of a vast empire, install drinking fountains made of lead in every entrance to their Coliseum? Most people today are unaware of that fact, as they are of lead's other benefits. Today, as always, lead's worst enemy is public ignorance. You might also remind the skeptical younger folks that fifty years ago, central nervous system damage was as common as hiccups—and taken about as seriously. Back then, if you had central nervous system damage, you didn't go looking for scapegoats among the heavy metals. You just changed into some loose-fitting clothing and went about your business—a prescription I am sure we would all find every bit as valid today.

Readers wishing a transcript of this column should sit down and copy it out in a firm hand on sheets of ruled paper. Then mail a check or money order for $12.99 to Hooker Publishing, 2,4,5-T Street, Niagara Falls, New York 13870.

MORRIS SMITH:
THE MAN AND THE MYTH

With a graceful tug, Dr. Morris Smith opens the venetian blinds. Light glints on his faceted forehead, on his metal-rimmed glasses, on the silvery medical instruments in the pocket of his white lab coat. Beyond his office door, he knows, is a waiting room filled with patients who all too soon will begin their ceaseless round of demands upon him. This will be the only time he has to himself for the rest of the day.

Just for a moment, Dr. Smith relaxes. He unbuttons his coat, turns on the coffee machine, leans back in his chair. Frequently charming and gregarious, Dr. Smith is nonetheless the kind of man who prefers the company of his own thoughts. He will always seem a bit alone no matter where he is, whether at a crowded cocktail party or in a darkened laboratory long after

his colleagues have gone home. His mind, trained
since youth in a discipline few men master, has developed the habit of solitude. At an age when most men
are barely ankle-deep in the waters of their chosen
careers, Dr. Smith has attained to such a position of
eminence in his field that a quick glance at the degrees
listed after his name in a medical directory does not
begin to tell the story. More than merely a professional, more, even, than a highly skilled specialist, Dr.
Smith is also a teacher, a counselor, a healer, a bearer
of the greatest hopes and darkest fears that dwell deep
inside us all.

With a sudden gesture, like a man awaking from a
reverie, Dr. Smith tosses off the last of his coffee. From
a desk drawer he takes a tall stack of patient files. He
searches the stack for a moment, finds the file he
wants, and bends over it at his desk with a concentra-
tion that seems to shut out the rest of the world. Another workday has begun for Dr. Morris Smith, prac-
ticing clinical sexologist.

My own acquaintance with Dr. Smith dates from over
a year ago, when I heard about his pioneering treatise
on harem pants. A lifelong fascination with the human
sciences prompted me to call him and request an interview. He readily agreed (asking only that I change
all identifying names, in the interest of his patients'
privacy; "Morris Smith" is, of course, a pseudonym).
A few days later, we met in the parking garage of the
major urban hospital where he practices. As he led me
into an elevator and down a series of corridors toward
the building's new fifty-million-dollar sexology wing,

I asked him what it was like to live inside the mythic image that surrounds his profession.

"It can be difficult, certainly," Dr. Smith said. "People see the sexologist as a man set apart, because of the godlike power he wields. But you must remember that there are many different kinds of sexologists. There are child sexologists, and adolescent sexologists, and sexogerontologists (sexologists who treat the elderly); some sexologists have large private practices, others operate mobile clinics in rural areas, and still others choose not to practice at all but, rather, devote their lives to a study of the vast literature of sexology."

An orderly wheeling a patient on a stretcher hurries across our path, and Dr. Smith stops short. Overhead, the hospital's public-address system urges its ceaseless petitions: *"Paging Dr. J . . . Dr. J, please report to Surgery at once . . . Dr. Severinsen . . . Dr. Severinsen, report to Emergency . . . Doc Severinsen to Emergency . . . Dr. No . . . Dr. No, please call your office . . ."* Nurses, interns, and hospital staff fill the halls with their purposeful bustle.

"So, you see, it's awfully hard to generalize about the profession as a whole," Dr. Smith continues. "The best you can do is to say that all sexologists are human beings, and I think it's important not only for the public but also for the sexologists themselves to try and keep that in mind. We're people, too. We put our pants on one leg at a time—and, of course, I should add that some of the greatest sexologists in history have been women."

A white-coated colleague waves a greeting as he passes, and Dr. Smith stops to introduce us. Then they begin to chat. I can pick out only the words "Spanish fly," "beautician," and "tilt-cup brassiere" before the conversation becomes too technical to follow.

Hours spent in office consultation with patients are what provide Dr. Smith with the raw data so important to his research and product-testing. He devotes four afternoons a week to these sessions, which he conducts in an atmosphere that is friendly, relaxed, and informal. Today, I will be observing him at work, and he takes a moment to brief me on his first patient. "This is a case which has so far resisted diagnosis," he says. "According to her history, her name is Andi, she's nineteen and a half years old, she's a Libra, she enjoys sketching, skiing, and sailing, she loves making love in the out-of-doors next to a babbling brook or on a windswept beach, she also loves to wear frilly underthings that her man can rip in bed, she can't stand smog, red meat, L.A. traffic, or pushy people, her favorite foreign movie is *Das Boot,* and she hopes someday for a career herself in movies. Her waist, hip, and bust readings are all better than normal for a girl her age, and to the untrained eye she would appear to be a picture of perfect sexual health. But in our previous sessions I have become convinced that something is deeply wrong—what, I don't know yet. Oh, one other note: Andi is basically a shy girl, but the camera turns her on. Unfortunately, I don't happen to have a camera with me today, so she's apt to be a bit withdrawn."

Dr. Smith's prediction proves accurate. The patient responds only with monosyllables to his inquiries, until, late in the session, she says that he doesn't un-

derstand, that she's "not like other girls." Encouraged
by this breakthrough, Dr. Smith pursues the point:
How, exactly, is she different? "Well, you see . . ." she
begins. A hot flush of shame colors her cheeks. "I've
never . . . I've never been even slightly attracted to a
man with a good sense of humor. In fact, that kind of
man repels me!"

Dr. Smith's face betrays no shock at this disclosure.
I think, How much he must have seen over the years!
In a soothing voice, he assures the patient that a dys-
function like hers, although rare, is not beyond treat-
ment. She leaves his office with a lighter step.

He wastes no time on self-congratulation. Instead,
I am surprised to see a sudden, uncharacteristic frown
cloud his features. "My next patient is in for some
rather bad news, I'm afraid," he says, reading the
question in my eyes. "It doesn't matter how many
sessions like this I go through, I never quite seem to
get used to them." He sighs, shakes his head, and then
presses the button on his intercom.

The patient, Mr. G., is a nondescript man wearing
glasses and crepe-soled shoes. Sweat beads his forehead, and his right hand toys with the paperweight
on the desk as he and Dr. Smith exchange small
talk. Finally, there comes a pause, and Mr. G. fixes
Dr. Smith with an intense stare. "O.K., Doc, give it
to me straight," he says. "How much longer have I
got?"

Unblinking, Dr. Smith returns his gaze. "Without
oral sex?" he says. "Possibly six months, possibly a
year."

Another pause. Mr. G. swallows hard, takes a deep
breath, and then expels it slowly. "Well . . ." he says,

"I guess knowing is better than not knowing. Right, Doc?"

When Mr. G. rises to leave, Dr. Smith is struck with a thought. Reaching into a drawer, he finds a lingerie catalogue from a department-store chain. "Mr. G., I want you to take this with you," he says. "If the pain becomes too severe, come back and I'll give you something stronger."

Outside the office windows, the spring sun shines down on the hospital courtyard, which is blooming with trees and shrubs in new leaf. Dr. Smith walks to a window and opens it. "Sometimes you can do so little," he says. "It's hard . . ." His voice trails off. Distant sounds—the twittering of birds, the high-pitched whine of a surgical saw, faint shouts of "Not that leg, you idiot!"—drift across the courtyard on the balmy air. The room begins to fill with the fragrance of new-mown grass and dogwood petals, and Dr. Smith breathes deeply. When he turns from the window, it is with the expression of a man whose peace of mind has been restored.

Marital counseling brings out the full spectrum of Dr. Smith's skills, and today his final appointment is with a couple who seem particularly troubled. The man, John, is in his mid-thirties, and wears a gray Glen-plaid suit. The woman, Barbara, is younger, dressed in a brown skirt and an orange smock. They are hardly in the door before the woman begins to protest that she must talk to Dr. Smith right away. Deftly, Dr. Smith takes control of the session: both partners will first tell their stories without interruption, he instructs, and then there will be time for discussion and evaluation.

Again Barbara protests; she is silenced by an admonitory finger. "John, please begin," Dr. Smith says.

JOHN'S STORY: "When Barbara and I met at a gallery opening in '71, it was a case of instant chemical attraction. We talked, we had a few glasses of wine, and then we took a taxi to my midtown apartment for a night of uninhibited lovemaking. The next morning we exchanged phone numbers, but, frankly, I never expected to see her again. I was very surprised and pleased several days later when I picked up the phone and heard her voice. This time, we met at her place for an encore, which, if anything, outdid our debut. We began to see each other regularly; after a few months, we moved in together, and in '74 we were married. Lawful domesticity did nothing to dampen our ardor —in fact, our performance in bed, like fine wine, only improved with age. Recently, however, there has been a change. Barbara has become cold and distant. Sometimes she ignores me for weeks, even months, at a time. She has a way of looking right through me that chills my blood. Perhaps the amount of time we both devote to our jobs is to blame; perhaps I am shutting her out of my life, just as she is shutting me out of hers, in a way that I can't see. All I know for sure is that I miss the magic we used to share, and I want, desperately, to get it back again."

Dr. Smith looks up from his notepad. "Now Barbara," he says.

BARBARA'S STORY: "Doctor, I have never seen this man before in my life. I haven't the faintest idea who he is, or why he has been bothering me all day. Not only are we not married, I don't even know the guy. The only way he knows my name is he read it off my

name tag. You must recognize me, Doctor. I'm a wait-
ress at the steak-and-ale place across the street. I
haven't been able to get a thing done with him always
following me around, trying to talk to me. He said he
was a patient of yours. Would you tell this man, who-
ever he is, that I'm not his wife, I'm not his friend, I've
never met him, I have no desire to meet him, and will
he please just leave me the hell alone!"

For a moment, Dr. Smith stares off into the distance,
the tips of his fingers touching. Then he says, "I've
often thought that marriage is rather like a tent. It
provides us with warmth and shelter, and yet the only
reason it stands at all is the many forces—the poles
and ropes and stakes—which pull it in different directions. When these forces are out of balance, when one
partner's push overpowers the other partner's pull, or
vice versa, that's when the tent of marriage begins to
collapse."

"Doctor, I am not married to him or anybody else!"
Barbara says, holding up her left hand. "See? No
ring!"

"Yes, Barbara, so you've stated. According to you,
you are not married; according to John, you and he
have been married for ten years. Isn't it reasonable to
assume that the truth must lie somewhere in between?"

"No! It isn't! Are you out of your mind? This man
has been harassing me!"

"Oh, Barbara, Barbara," John says.

In a rage, she turns on him. "Listen, if you come
within fifty feet of me again, I'm calling the police!
Understand? My God, you are all insane!" She leaves
the office at a run, slamming the door behind her.

We sit in silence for perhaps half a minute. "Go to her, John. Find her. Talk to her," Dr. Smith says softly.

"When I married Morris, I didn't just marry a man, I married a career," Mrs. Smith says, passing me the silver gravy boat. I am sitting at the family's dinner table in their comfortable split-level home. Across the table sit the Smiths' two sons, aged nine and thirteen, and on my right is the Smiths' attractive sixteen-year-old daughter.

"If it weren't for you, I'd still be working in my parents' shop in Times Square," Dr. Smith says, smiling back at his wife over the candlelight.

Hesitantly, with an affecting shyness, Dr. Smith has allowed me greater and greater glimpses of the private man, glimpses that confirm what I had long suspected: his success has never lacked for support from a remarkable and understanding family.

"He's a pretty great dad, really," says the younger son.

"Yeah, he always brings us neat stuff from his office. Anatomically correct dolls and stuff," the older one puts in.

"He's not an old bluenose with hidebound views of sexual morality, like some of my boyfriends' dads," the daughter adds.

Embarrassed by this praise, Dr. Smith smiles down at the slice of roast on his plate.

"When your husband is in a demanding, high-risk job, you learn to love him when you can," Mrs. Smith says. "And you learn how to let go. If he didn't live for that big, shiny clinic of his, he wouldn't be Morris, and if he weren't Morris I guess I wouldn't love him."

"It's been hard for you, I know," Dr. Smith murmurs.

"Every time he walks in that door, I say a little prayer. And every time he walks out I pray that he'll walk back in again. Every time that phone rings, I think it's the hospital calling to tell me that something's happened to Morris, that something's gone wrong with one of his experiments, that Morris has been—" Her brave smile has begun to tremble around the edges.

"Now, dear, you know I take every precaution."

"I know, but when I think of that colleague of yours in Sweden, that horrible accident with the vibrating chair . . ." She blinks at the tears as her voice catches.

"Really, dear, you mustn't—"

"Isn't this silly of me," she says, brushing at her eyes with her napkin. "Oh, I'll be all right in a minute."

Suddenly the beeper Dr. Smith wears at his belt makes an insistent noise. The family takes no notice as he excuses himself and heads for the telephone; over the years, such interruptions have become as much a part of their mealtimes as the clink of sterling on china. When Dr. Smith returns, he is no longer the relaxed father enjoying a quiet evening at home. "That was the Governor's personal bodyguard," he says in a voice flat with urgency. "The Governor has become . . ."

"Impotent?" Mrs. Smith asks, going white under her tan.

"That's the preliminary indication."

"Oh, my God!"

"They're sending a chopper in ten minutes to fly me to the capital," Dr. Smith says.

"Quickly, children," Mrs. Smith says. "Take flashlights and stand out on the lawn, so they can see where to land."

The next few minutes pass like speeded-up film as Mrs. Smith packs a lunch for her husband, finds him a warm sweater, helps him with his raincoat. The sound of rotor blades can be heard descending from above.

"Good luck, Morris," Mrs. Smith calls after him, holding up two sets of crossed fingers.

Halfway through the door, he turns and comes back to her. "You know something? You're pretty wonderful yourself," he says, giving her a quick kiss.

Dr. Smith runs across the lawn, bathed in landing lights, to the open helicopter door. One hand holds his hat on his head against the downwash; the other hand clutches an emergency kit of arousal aids. He pulls the door shut, the noise of the engine rises, and then the machine swings up into the night sky.

"Good luck, Daddy! We love you!" the children cry.

Transfixed, we all follow the lights until they vanish over the tree line on their mission of hope. Darkness and quiet return; on the lawn, the flattened blades of grass unbend. For the loved ones Dr. Smith must leave behind, the hardest part—the waiting—has begun.

ENGLAND PICKS A POET

In England, when people discuss poetry they're talking business—big business. Some countries leave their poets gathering dust on the academic shelf, but here in England people like their poetry the way they like their tea: hot, fresh, and three times a day. Poetry experts estimate that in one fiscal year the English poetic community generates over 950 million pounds (almost 1.2 billion dollars) in revenue, all of which goes right back into the local economy. That works out to about twenty-six dollars apiece for every English man, woman, and child. With numbers like these, it's no wonder that poets here demand, and receive, the highest word rate of any Western country.

At the top of this heap sits the poet laureate of England. Chosen from among the best in his field, the poet laureate is a throwback to the days of the royal bard, constantly singing odes at the jeweled elbow of some pagan king. Today, the poet laureate no longer spends all his time around the palace but is permitted to live in his own style of home and furnish it as he wishes. This, combined with a salary, income from lectures and endorsements, and the unlimited use of a government vehicle, makes the job one of the most attractive in all literature. So when Queen Elizabeth and Prime Minister Thatcher announced earlier this year that they were looking for a new person for the post, they received so many applications that they have already been forced to pull a couple of all-nighters in an attempt to read through them. Fueled by innumerable cigarettes and cups of coffee, the Queen and the Prime Minister have checked and double-checked every poem and application, always with this dark thought at the back of their minds: What if we make a mistake?

As students of history, they know how costly human error can be. Sometimes it has meant that the foremost living poet missed his chance to be laureate, as happened this century with W. H. Auden. After getting the necessary recommendations and breezing through a personal interview with King George VI, Auden, who had the highest Q rating of any poet in the world, looked like a certainty. But he neglected to make the important post-interview follow-up call, and then the King misplaced Auden's folder when he went on vacation and didn't know how to get in touch with him. The loss to literature resulting from this act of carelessness can only be imagined.

Other poets appear to be qualified during the selection process and then, once installed, they turn into complete goldbricks. That was what William Words-worth did. From our vantage point of years, we can see that Wordsworth's entire career was nothing but an elaborate bait-and-switch scam: write some poetry, get yourself chosen poet laureate, and then—quittin' time! In Wordsworth's years as laureate, he became so bone-lazy that he would write only the meters of poems; he would do a limerick:

> De duh de de duh de de *dah,*
> De duh de de duh de de *dah.*
> De duh de de duh,
> De duh de de duh,
> De duh de de duh de de *dah.*

Then he would mail that in to the "Information, Please" column of the London *Times Literary Supplement* and ask if any subscriber knew what the words might be.

Just as disappointing was Alfred, Lord Tennyson, a laureate who literally could not write his way out of a paper bag. He proved this at a benefit performance for the Christian Temperance League in 1879. The poet was placed inside a large sack of standard-weight brown paper on a stage at Covent Garden, given several pens, and left to himself. He thrashed and flopped helplessly inside for four and a half hours; finally, members of the Grenadier Guards had to come and cut him free.

How Tennyson ever made laureate is anybody's guess, yet even he was an improvement on John Dry-den, England's first poet laureate, although by no means her best. Whenever people told Dryden they didn't like one of his poems, he threw such a fit—arguing, sulking, and snapping at them—that they would resolve never to be candid with him again. By means of such behavior, Dryden was able, in a short period of time, to manipulate an entire population into pretending that he was a genius without equal. Today, we know better.

And what of John Masefield, poet laureate from 1930 to 1967? He was the one, you will remember, who penned the howler "Sea Fever," with the opening

> I must go down to the seas again,
> to the lonely sea and the sky

Eeeeeeeouch! It is a sad fact that among past poets laureate of England tin ears like Masefield's have been not the exception but the rule.

If anyone can turn this tradition around, Queen Elizabeth and Prime Minister Thatcher can. Both have proved themselves to be smart, articulate women with an eye for spotting talent—and the world of contemporary poetry gives them quite a bit of talent to spot. So far, the top candidates are Philip Larkin, 62; Roy Fuller, 72; D. J. Enright, 64; Gavin Ewart, 68; Ted Hughes, 53; and Dr. Leo Buscaglia, 59. Larkin is a popular essayist, as well as a poet with a strong sense of the beauties of commonplace speech. Fuller served on the governing board of the BBC, England's main TV network, and a reflected glow from that "cool medium" often shines through the luminous poetry on which his reputation rests. Both Enright and Ewart have been poets since they were very little, and they have had a great many interesting insights over the years. Hughes is a much-honored poet whose trademark is the originality shown in every page of his work, which combines a love for the rhythms of nature with some other values. Buscaglia, though not, strictly speaking, a poet or an Englishman, still might be as good a choice as anyone, if not better. First, he is a doctor; second, he is an author and expert on the subject of human emotion, notably love, which has always been the poet's province; and third, his books, *Love,* and *Living, Loving, and Learning,* and *Personhood,* which have sold in the millions, are profound enough to be poetry already. With a slight change in typography, they would be. Lots of people know who Dr. Buscaglia is. And, compared to more traditional poets, Dr. Buscaglia is a nicer person. He could infuse social functions with a warm feeling that would humanize all that glittering pomp, and everyone would benefit. Along with poetic talent, the ability to reach out to others might well be an important requirement for the poet laureate of the future.

Soon the Queen and the Prime Minister will announce their decision. One of the candidates will wear the wreath of laurel; the rest will send their congratulations, and console themselves with the thought that, at this level of poetry, there really are no losers. With a new poet laureate at the helm, a new era in English poetry may dawn. And in libraries and country retreats and book-lined dens across the land thousands of poets will return to their work, providing the verse that feeds a nation.

A NOTE FROM
THE PLAYWRIGHT

To the theatergoer: The performance of *Songs for a Conquered Moon* that you are about to see differs so completely from the spirit of the play as I wrote it that I wish hereby to disavow any and all association between myself and this production. If I could, I would remove my name from the marquee and from the program you hold in your hands; unfortunately, I am informed by my lawyers that contractual considerations render this impossible. When I wrote *Songs,* I set out to weave a net of speech, action, and mood with which to ensnare certain moments in human existence that are as fleeting and evanescent as a dream. Seeing my lovely net filled instead with the unappetizing aesthetic baggage of one particular director and set of actors makes me wonder briefly why I ever chose this regrettable profession in the first place.

My carefully crafted stage directions, absolutely essential to any understanding of the play, have been discarded from this production with a thoroughness that suggests the hired vandal. The freeway pile-up in the middle of Act II has mysteriously disappeared, without an explanation; the chorus of forty Greek sailors commenting on the action has been replaced by two town criers (obviously not Greek); the underwater sequences have been crudely faked; and the marvelous moment at the climax of Act III, when Lord Hargreaves draws his breath to sneeze and his starched shirtfront rolls up under his nose like a window shade, has been so toned down as to lose all its impact. I could continue this list almost endlessly . . . But really, why bother?

Now, as per the agreement between my attorneys and the attorneys for the Top Contemporary Theater Company, I include here the first few pages of *Songs for a Conquered Moon,* exactly as they were written. I hope that they will give some idea of the very great distance between my play as it was originally intended and the shabby counterfeit you see on the stage before you.

SONGS FOR
A CONQUERED MOON
A Play in Three Acts

Cast of Characters

Marcelline, a woman so beautiful it is impossible to look at her without a sharp intake of breath. A strong woman whose looks are a form of disguise; beneath those high-fashion dresses hides an adventurous tomboy with many of the same traits as her father, a billionaire.

John Vanderjohn, a third-generation brain surgeon and outsider. Wears his hair a bit overlong, down to and beyond his shirt collar. The echo of an Old World patronymic in his name is intentional; he should suggest the epic proportions of a Tolstoy, wandering lost in this shopkeepers' century.

Railroad Tom Stevens, a poet, a prophet, a preacher, a liar. A man as full of contradictions as the nightly news. He'd give his last quarter to a little boy, and then change his mind. Also, he is able to "shape-shift"—change from human form to that of any other species—in a matter of seconds. Lover to Pamela.

One Stab, a full-blooded Indian. Silent, laconic, terse, and as violent as the occasion requires. Well over seven feet tall. Mr. Earl's factotum.

Mark Brainard, a young writer and critic with the most brilliant mind of his generation.

Bob, a neighbor from downstairs.

Five Claims Adjusters
The "Solid Gold" Dancers
Assorted Messengers and Passersby
Some Other People

Act I

The time is the present, approximately.

The setting is anywhere along the Pacific rim; state or country need not be made explicit. Set designers are referred to postcards of the region, Kabuki drawings, and the imitation–French Regency landscaping favored by gangsters and the newly famous. A western pine perhaps, stunted bonsai-style, clinging to a coastal rock. Stage right, there is a fifty-foot waterfall, and at stage left we see an eight-lane suspension bridge of reinforced concrete. In the background is an active volcano, with molten lava coming down the sides and slowly making its way to the footlights. Overhead a real airport control tower broods above the scene.

The lighting should try for an effect both spare and lush, if possible. It should change almost continually, as the moment dictates. For the second act the light panel must be equipped with at least four state-of-the-art military lasers. Interacting with the cast members and the scenery, the lighting will become practically like another character in the drama, as palpable as the charmed radiance in a painting by Raphael or Giotto or someone of equal stature.

JOHN *is seated in a chair downstage right. The residue of a black mood can still be seen around the corners of his eyes. Occasionally he knits his brow and shakes his head. Close at hand is a fresh cup of imported coffee, which he sips from time to time.* MARCELLINE *enters stage left.*

MARCELLINE [*hauntingly*]: Oh, hi, John.

JOHN [*in an upsetting tone*]: Oh, hi, Marcelline. How come you're right here?

MARCELLINE [*movingly*]: I just came in from over where I was.

JOHN [*no longer depressed*]: Oh, that's great!

MARCELLINE [*affectingly*]: So, what if we—

JOHN [*expressing the audience's hidden fears*]: Wait, wait, no—

MARCELLINE [*with perfect timing*]: Hear me out.

JOHN [*in his regular voice*]: O.K.

MARCELLINE [*compellingly*]: What if we went to a store and bought some things?

JOHN [*after a pause of twenty-four seconds*]: Oh, O.K.

The scene then shifts to Tibet. MARCELLINE *and* JOHN *come in.* TOM *is already there.*

TOM [*instantly commanding attention*]: Hi, you guys.

MARCELLINE [*responding to what* TOM *has said*]: Hi.

JOHN: Hi, Tom.

TOM [*memorably*]: What do you say we go and get something to eat?

MARCELLINE [*with a touching expression*]: Thanks. I'd like that.

    JOHN [*this is a great line*]: Count me in.

    TOM [*excitingly*]: O.K., let's go!

I am sorry that, owing to limitations of space, this excerpt cannot be longer. I would suggest that those of you as yet unfamiliar with my work go out and buy copies of all my plays, the better to judge future productions for yourselves. And I would also ask that the next time you want to see a play by me, you call me first to ask whether the production is any good or not. (I am home most evenings, and if I'm out, someone can take a message.) I know full well that a writer's relationship with his audience is the most important one he has. After all, without you, where would I be? I would even go to your houses, no matter how long it would take to see everybody. If you have any questions, I would welcome the opportunity to sit down with each of you on an individual basis to discuss just how great my play could have been.

Your Notes

Notes

Notes

Notes

Notes

Notes

Notes

Notes

Notes

Notes